# imperfect balance

### BEHAVIORAL HEALTH DISORDERS
### &
### FIRST YEAR MEDICAL STUDENTS

*The narratives shared in this book highlight the lives of ten first-year medical students, each of whom has struggled and continues to struggle with a behavioral health disorder. Their stories were transcribed from the podcasts of fellow student, Logan Noone. The interviews took place in the Spring Semester of 2018, halfway through Year One.*

© Copyright 2019, by Richard Arroyo & Logan Noone

All rights reserved, including the right of reproduction in whole or in part in any form. No part of this publication may be reproduced, distributed or transmitted in any form or by any means without the prior written permission of the authors, except in certain non-commercial uses permitted by copyright law.

This is a work of nonfiction. Some names and locations have been changed.

*To those who are struggling*
 *and persist*

**D.O.**     Doctor of Osteopathic Medicine
**OMS-I**   First-Year Osteopathic Medical Student


The students who are recounting their struggles and successes within these pages are first-year osteopathic medical students attending medical school in the Pacific Northwest United States.

Doctors of Osteopathic Medicine, D.O.'s, are equivalent to Doctors of Allopathic Medicine, M.D.'s. Both schools of medicine graduate physicians who can specialize in any field, prescribe medications, perform surgeries, and practice medicine within the United States. Both are required to sit for national board exams and meet the standards determined by their respective national medical associations. There is now even an integration of the residency selection process and accreditation for D.O. and M.D. Resident Physicians.

Osteopathic medical education emphasizes a holistic approach toward the treatment of patients. That is to say, there are factors beyond physical disease or illness alone that we are taught to consider which influence patient health. We are taught to observe our patients, considering psychological influences, to uncover the root causation of symptoms. We are instructed in osteopathic techniques with the understanding that dysfunction in one part of the body, mind, and spirit can influence any other part of the person. This is where a holistic perspective allows osteopathic physicians to look beyond pharmaceuticals as the exclusive cure to all maladies.

We cannot simply categorize people by disease or disorder. Some of the students in this collection choose to take medication whereas others do not. Each individual is unique, seeking treatment with different types of therapy, striving to achieve both personal and academic goals.

As this is a work of nonfiction, do not feel confined to the order of the chapters.

# INDEX

Foreword, by Logan Noone ......................................... 1

Medical School. What Is It Really Like? ...................... 11

Behavioral Health Disorders in Medical School ......... 23

---

### FIRST YEAR MEDICAL STUDENTS:

LOGAN ............................................................... 33
*bipolar disorder*

MEGAN .............................................................. 61
*obsessive-compulsive disorder;*
*attention-deficit hyperactivity disorder*

NEELOU ............................................................. 87
*general anxiety disorder; panic disorder*

AUGUSTUS ....................................................... 101
*attention-deficit hyperactivity disorder*

DANIELLA ........................................................ 117
*major depressive disorder; postpartum depression*

LAURA .............................................................. 141
*general anxiety disorder; major depressive disorder;*
*graves' disease*

TED .................................................................. 163
*attention-deficit hyperactivity disorder*

HEATHER ......................................................... 177
*sexual assault survivor; general anxiety disorder;*
*major depressive disorder; ADHD*

JUSTIN .............................................................. 199
*post-traumatic stress disorder*

RICHARD .......................................................... 215
*undiagnosed; child of paranoid schizophrenic*

---

Medical School. First Year Finally Wrapping Up ........ 241

Endnotes ................................................................. 249

*Am I Too Screwed Up For This?*

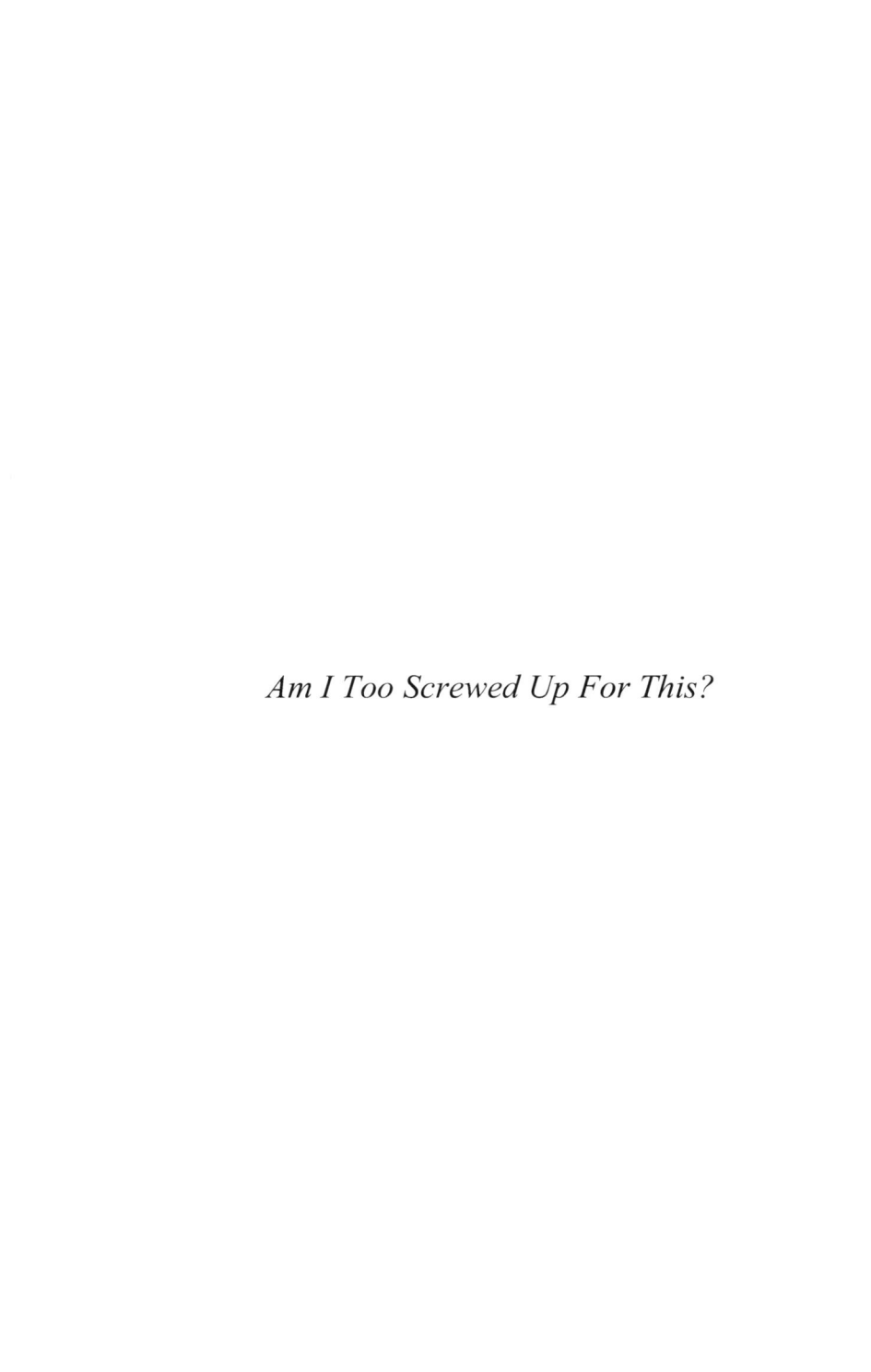

# FOREWORD
## BY LOGAN NOONE

I'll never forget the whirlwind of emotions I felt walking into medical school on day one of orientation. I was over-the-moon excited, but I felt as though I didn't belong. The admissions committee must have made a mistake. I had a lingering fear that I wasn't smart enough to be here. A tornado of euphoria and anxiety consumed me as I walked into the big lecture hall.

# 2

"Pleasure to meet you," a deep voice with a hint of southern twang greeted me. "My name is Richard."

He was the first classmate I met at orientation and I did my best to sound friendly and respectful, but my mind continued to race. We were in the middle of conventional introductions like 'where are you from,' and 'how was your trip here,' when I apologized to Richard.

"I'm sorry," I said. "I can barely talk right now. I still can't believe I actually made it here." I think I had a big, goofy grin on my face. Richard had no idea what I was referring to, but the past five years of my life involved me leaving a career in insurance, becoming a public speaker, enrolling in science classes at a community college, and moving back and forth across the United States – but strangely, my journey to medical school began after I was admitted into a psych ward. And so walking into the big lecture hall, I felt I was the odd duck in a room full of new medical students. I assumed all of my new classmates were cookie-cutter, straight-A, cancer-research kinds of students. It didn't take me long to realize how wrong I was.

"Me neither," Richard said. "Between you and me, this was the only school that even interviewed me. I just got off the waitlist last month. It still hasn't hit me yet that I'm even here."

Richard was a career-changing student too. He got his start in law school. It was comforting knowing I wasn't the only nontraditional medical student. This initial conversation started a strong bond between us. Through the struggles of the first overwhelming months, we tried our best to help each other academically; mostly, though, we supported each other emotionally. I constantly thought I was going to flunk out. Fifty-thousand dollars in tuition down the drain, the embarrassment, lack of self-confidence – these thoughts and feelings raced through my head night after night.

My desire to pursue medicine stems from my decision to live openly with my bipolar disorder. I believe mental health conditions are easier to manage when you feel supported by the community around you. Prior to medical school, I worked as a mental health public speaker, sharing my story at hospitals, colleges, and at fundraisers. I loved the impact my story would have on an audience. I could help others feel more comfortable dealing with their own behavioral health challenges. But I learned that I got the most satisfaction by talking with people from the audience after my speech.

Although I'm not the most academically gifted of my peers, I just might be the loudest. I don't hide my bipolar disorder. It is a big part of who I am. Interestingly, over the course of first semester, other students started approaching me about their own mental health challenges. They seemed to feel more comfortable knowing they weren't alone with their struggles. I realized that I wasn't the only medical student who lived with mental illness – in fact, far from it.

It had become a tradition to have a celebratory beer with Richard after passing a course by the skin of our teeth. It was during this first semester when we both realized our affinity for psychiatry. We acknowledged that one of the biggest problems in mental health is convincing people to speak up. Talk to your doctor. Talk to your family. Talk to your friends. There is a stigma surrounding mental health, but by talking about it we can start to change it.

Now, I have always been an avid podcast listener. I even took part as a guest on a few podcasts. I must say, I was intrigued by the idea of starting my own podcast; however, I was reluctant to take the leap and take on so big a commitment. It was over a celebratory beer when Richard changed my mind.

"Stop focusing on your own experience. Think about the audience. People feel comforted hearing your story, and so imagine sharing all kinds of stories, all kinds of mental health triumphs."

I had been thinking about starting a podcast for years; I just never had the confidence to take the leap. But here I was in medical school, in the bliss of having just passed Cardiology, when I finally decided to do it – and *Talk Mental Health with Logan Noone* was born.

Medical school consumes your entire life. Relationships fall to the wayside. Hobbies are forgotten. Creativity wanes. Podcasting, for me, has allowed me to compartmentalize the academic load and use my mind in other aspects of my life. Because I'm in medical school, my classmates became my first guests. These interviews gave me the opportunity to learn about them on a deep and intimate level. Our conversations strayed from our academics to our lives, difficulties, obstacles, successes and struggles. I felt creative again. Podcasting has helped put my life back into perspective. I can't give one-hundred percent of myself to study. I have to develop and maintain the other parts of my life too. I am more successful in this state of balance.

From the very start, Richard saw how the podcast was impacting my life. He suggested that it could shape my practice of psychiatry one day. He also agreed to be a regular guest on the show and even gave me suggestions on how to be a better interviewer, and more importantly, a better listener. Then one day he came with another suggestion. You see, Richard isn't a person who listens to podcasts, and he assumed that there are many others who don't and probably never will. "You can reach a bigger audience if you change the medium for presenting these stories, because it's not important how these stories reach people – what's important is *that* they reach people."

One theme that has emerged from each story is how every individual has managed their mental health better after having confided in somebody, and the person they confided to didn't have to be a psychologist or psychiatrist. The notion that mental health management must necessarily begin with a 'professional' is one of the barriers keeping people from opening up. It reinforces the stigma of mental health. By simply opening up to a friend, a family member, or a mentor, each of the guests on my show – and me too, definitely me too – we were able to start the long process of healing.

L. N.

*December 26, 2018*

8

*Imperfect Balance*

# MEDICAL SCHOOL
## WHAT IS IT REALLY LIKE?

*It's like trying to drink water from a fire hydrant* – this is the classic analogy to illustrate the difficulty of medical school. But it's a lie. Medical school is not a fire hydrant; it's a tsunami. And I am running as fast as I can to survive. I can't stop running and I can't slow down. Then it barrels down upon me, sweeps me off my feet, churns me and draws me into a deep, dark place. I kick and paddle furiously. I reach my arms out for anything. If I can just reach the surface for a breath of air, I can keep going a little longer.

I must not lose myself to the panic.

THOSE OF US who share our stories within these pages are first-year medical students studying osteopathic medicine. We all knew upon entering into this career path that it would be difficult. Besides those student outliers who seem to sail right over the storm, it is even more difficult than we expected. Nearly every moment is dedicated to study, and yet I never feel adequately prepared. I need to sleep, but it would be unreasonable to stop studying just to sleep. I need to keep myself socially grounded, but it would be irresponsible to go out for fun when I have so much to do. For some of us – those of us with diagnosed or undiagnosed behavioral health disorders – the high-stress, high-stakes academic struggle aggravates and amplifies our emotional struggle.

*Where you might be feeling lonely, you feel neglected and forgotten.*

*Where you might be feeling anxious, you feel despair and hopelessness.*

Being a medical student is a paradox. I love it, but this has been one of the more difficult years of my life – and possibly the most distressing to my emotional health. I *think* I'm happy, but then happiness is relative to the next exam or major deadline. This happiness usually lasts no more than a week, or more commonly, a few days. Of course, while in the sloshing of incessant study and the emotional seasickness of endless academia, I am quite miserable. But when I make myself step back and look upon the panorama of the storm – you see, I have dreamt of being a medical student for a very long time, and I didn't think I was capable of making it here – then, yes, it feels something like happiness. But it doesn't last long. I have a test to study for.

\* \* \*

First year medical school is typically an eight-to-five school day with an hour for lunch that is often filled with an optional guest lecture or club event. There are also the tutoring sessions, exam reviews, required community outings, papers to write, online modules to complete, and most importantly – you have to make time to actually learn the material. It is not uncommon to stay at school until early morning. Many students leave campus the moment lecture ends. Others don't attend class at all; instead, they watch lectures on double-speed from their computers at home, only showing up for quizzes, exams, and other required events. There are many ways to be a successful medical student.

Time is the great antagonist of the medical student. There is simply never enough. I attend all lectures – yet I often wonder if my efforts would be better spent by using those many hours for self-learning. I tend to stay on campus and sequester myself into a study cubby, forcing a break every two hours to step outside or pace the halls. If you stay late enough, you'll find a student hunched over in delicate sleep, clutching notes or a laptop. Brush too close and she or he will jolt with a look of momentary confusion followed by sharp focus, conscious of the dwindling time.

*THE CURRICULUM:*

Educational objectives are standardized across medical schools. Each school, however, is unique in how it chooses to present that curriculum to its students. This is the structure of the first-year curriculum at my medical school; and although the struggle of each student is distinct, we try to portray the effort so that others can understand the daily obstacles and triumphs.

The academia begins with an intensive and comprehensive review of the undergraduate sciences compiled into a single sixteen-week course, titled *Foundations of Medicine*. Each one-hour lecture is the equivalent academic load of two weeks in an upper-level undergraduate science class, and on any given day we would have two to five of these lectures. Outside of basic lecture, we had microscopy projects, personal nutritional and wellness analysis, and the dreaded self-evaluations. Students were often assigned to random groups for pathology analysis and practical pathophysiology, looking beyond patterns of disorders and truly investigating the why and the how. Countless quizzes, team projects, and five high-stakes exams made this course a shocking beginning to the storm.

The academic year likewise begins with Anatomy – a year-long course with both a lecture and a laboratory component. Similar to *Foundations of Medicine,* there are one-hour anatomy lectures peppered throughout the week, and regular high-stake exams and quizzes. Each lecture is extremely dense and designed to correlate to the lab component of the course. And, yes, anatomy lab is exactly how you imagine it: from that initial slice through the skin of the upper back on day one to ultimately holding a human brain in your hands, marveling at its weight and size, the organ that once housed the soul and memories of our first patient. Students are assigned in groups of four to a cadaver, with groups redistributed every month as we begin the dissection of a new body system. The exam component of anatomy lab consists of forty cadavers with a small pin inserted into either a muscle, nerve, artery, vein, layer of fascia, connective tissue, or an arrow pointing at a seemingly arbitrary notch or curve on a bone, or any of a countless number of fissures or prominences or convexities no more subjectively significant than a noodle in a pool of noodles; physiologically, however, each structure serves a distinct purpose and is vital to the proper functioning of the human body. *Anything's game* is what our professors say. Students have thirty seconds to write down the name of the pinned structure before cycling to the next station. Anatomy is the quintessential medical school course and the cadavers are regarded as our first patients and treated thus with absolute dignity.

Osteopathic Principles and Philosophy (OPP) is a year-long course unique to osteopathic medicine. The course, much like anatomy, is divided into two-hour lectures and three-hour laboratory components each week. OPP is the primary distinction between the D.O. and M.D. medical education. The practice of osteopathic manipulation involves diagnosing somatic (body) dysfunction using palpatory skills and assessing for tenderness, asymmetries, restrictions of motion, and tissue texture abnormalities. The second component is learning to apply various physical techniques to balance and correct the dysfunction. Often overlooked and underappreciated, osteopathic manipulation is a form of treatment that can profoundly improve and sometimes restore a patient's physical health and comfort.

Clinical Skills is another year-long course that emphasizes the clinical practice of medicine, such as learning how to take an appropriate patient history, how to perform a proper physical exam, and how to write an objective patient evaluation, assessment and plan. We practice various physical exam techniques upon our colleagues in laboratory sessions. Then we incorporate what we learned into standardized patient encounters with patient-actors in timed settings where we are expected to evaluate a chief complaint and discuss the differential diagnoses and plan with the patient. Following our encounter, we submit a written subjective and objective assessment and plan. We also perform simulated emergency encounters where student teams perform in groups of four, cycling students through designated roles such as team leader, task performer, historian, and scribe. Practiced tasks include intubation, IV insertions, and catheter placement. The simulation itself is carried out in a mock emergency room upon a rather frightening automaton that blinks, talks, convulses, and has dynamic vital signs that respond to ordered procedures and medications – and, of course, the SIM-man can tragically die if and when the team screws up.

Art and Practice of Doctoring is another year-long course. It is unique in that it exposes the students to relevant social issues, active community projects, available governmental programs, as well as cultural norms and societal disparities in medicine. The aim of the course is to develop students into better-informed and more well-rounded physicians. Throughout the year, we are required to attend various community outings. For instance, I accompanied a hospice worker and visited a terminally ill patient at his home. Another time, I sat in on a group therapy session at a drug rehabilitation center. The course often hosts guest speakers who lecture on a variety of relevant topics ranging from how primary care physicians can help identify sex trafficked victims, how to communicate effectively with war veterans, and how to appreciate the culture of the deaf. It is a meaningful course, allowing us to be human, and provides a retreat from the basic sciences.

To conclude the foundational classes, Introduction to Pharmacology is an eleven-week course constructed to teach students the general drug classes, methods of action, adverse effects and contraindications of various medications. The course is taught by a tall professor, part mad scientist, with almost every letter after his name for the accolades he has gained throughout his very diverse career. Though we have only sat in these chairs of medicine for a short time, he always addresses us as *Doctor* when calling on us to answer questions. This course is designed to conclude alongside *Foundations of Medicine,* giving students only a short respite before the next step. After the final exams for the introductory courses, there is a weekend break before students must apply their foundational knowledge into each body system.

*SYSTEMS-BASED COURSES:*

Some medical schools categorize classes via the traditional basic sciences, such as Pathology,

Biochemistry, Physiology, Pharmacology, etc. A systems-based medical education, alternatively, consolidates all the basic sciences of each specific system of the body, such as Musculoskeletal, Cardiology, Pulmonology, etc., to allow students to better integrate foundational sciences and clinical education. The three systems listed – those which my school has chosen to integrate into its first-year curriculum – are each grueling and complex. Cardiology, for instance, is one of the more dreaded courses; so is Renal, a Second-Year course. The systems courses typically consist of two to three exams and a slew of quizzes. Just as students finally figured out the rhythm for *Foundations of Medicine*, the curriculum challenges them to change how they study for each new system. At this point, the pace of learning is accelerated as each system is only six to eight weeks in length and each exam can make or break a student.

*EXAMS:*

You leave your bag with your phone turned off at the front of the lecture hall. It is the same lecture hall where we spend the majority of every day, but there is an especially heavy air before each exam. Some students are quizzing each other. Others are quietly reviewing notes on a laptop. Some students appear in a daze as though they did not sleep at all. Others perform rituals in the minutes before the exam begins. One girl walks the rows with an expression of profound gravity upon her face and shakes hands with each student one after another and wishes them good luck. These exams comprise the majority of points for each course. Because of the abundance of material tested, it is uncommon to feel wholly and adequately prepared.

The exam proctor begins making the usual announcements. *There are no restroom breaks allowed because this exam is under two hours.* You put your ear buds in and the proctor's voice becomes muffled and distant. *Good luck everybody. You may begin the exam.* You enter a password into the secured exam program on your computer. Sheets of scratch paper are passed down the row. Some students close their eyes and whisper what I assume is a prayer. The lecture hall is absolutely silent now and the students are entering into trance-like states of resolve and conviction. There is a countdown clock at the top right of the screen. You have to move through the exam at an intentional pace to finish on time. An hour passes before you realize that your eyes are dry because you haven't blinked.

When the clock expires, or you simply click *Submit*, the secured program takes a few seconds to process your score – the anxiety in these seconds is wrenching. This is when seconds feel like hours and your mind races. *I might have bombed this one. I need a 66% to pass this class. Is it okay to cry?* A raw score pops up and is a number like 89/133. You try to do the math in your head. You have been in a test-taking trance for hours. It is a gradual reemergence.

Outside of the lecture hall, students are jubilant and eating the densest brownies made by our mad scientist professor. The sweetness of the brownies snaps you out of your trance. It is the cycle of studying, projects, anxiety, sleep-deprivation, exams and brownies that is the oscillating tsunami of first year medical school. I paddle furiously and take a deep breath of air before I am again submerged beneath the waves.

# BEHAVIORAL HEALTH DISORDERS
## IN MEDICAL SCHOOL

*Why are some minds so perfect and mine so flawed?*
*If my mind is flawed, I too must be flawed.*
*My 'self' is flawed.*

*Does this mean that I am damaged?*

OUR MINDS are in perpetual conflict. The stresses upon the average medical student – fear, drive, urgency, vulnerability, hope colliding with failures and successes – are intense and powerful stressors. Such stressors are known triggers of behavioral health disorders.

The students of my class exhibit a spectrum of both diagnosed and undiagnosed behavioral health disorders. Some thrive in the high stress environment of medical school; others constantly struggle. Some suffer compounding anxiety because of the unrelenting demands of school; alternatively, some students are capable of harnessing their symptoms and channeling them toward an objective. Surely there are students who are suffering silently, choosing to hide their mental health anguish; others are staunch advocates for their respective conditions. Some of us are just trying to get through today, convinced that *tomorrow* will be better, *next week* will be even better, *next month* will be wonderful because first year will finally conclude, and *next year* will be amazing if I can only become a second-year medical student. Some students are having the time of their lives right now. I have fleeting moments of this too, although medical school for me is mostly a terrifying and grueling experience.

This is what I often experience –

While studying, my focus will divert and fixate on something trivial. It is probably a scapegoat for my insecurities and resentments. *My brother hates me. I loathe that person. These aren't my people. I am too different. I don't belong. They made a mistake accepting me.* It can be devastating to succumb to such unchecked emotions. Is my mind simply protecting itself from the strain of study by finding trivial things to divert my attention toward?

What is the mind but our perceptions processed into self-awareness? While the brain is a physical organ, the mind is an essence: an accumulation of the senses. The mind influences (i) how we act, (ii) how we feel, and (iii) who we *think* we are. And if the mind is the structured interpretation of our senses, and if it is regulated by hormones produced within our bodies, then the maintenance of our hormones is instrumental to our sense-of-self: how we act, how we feel, and who we *think* we are.

For some of us, however, the fulcrum upon which our hormones are balanced can shift. Emotions can tilt askew. Our minds can deceive us. This is the trap of a behavioral health disorder.

\* \* \*

The process of getting accepted into medical school is arduous and complicated. At the time that I was applying, I believed it excessive. The application process alone is an obstacle course designed to shake off everyone but the most steadfast. Two years of undergraduate science prerequisite coursework. Letters of recommendation from both science professors and physicians. An implicit requirement of hands-on medical experience. Numerous essays to write, followed by a second batch of even more specific essays to write. Thousands of dollars in application fees and travel expenses. And then, if you are fortunate enough to be offered an interview at a school, let alone multiple interviews, each will be a day-long process of being scrutinized alongside the most impressive academic candidates nation-wide.

I am only now beginning to understand the logic for such an arduous and complicated application process.

There is a specific trait which every medical student in my first-year class possesses. It is difficult to define, as each student has a character that is unique and perceptible, but I will generally label it as intermingling *maturity, empathy,* and *tenacity* – I call it *grit*.

Every medical student I have encountered has shown a capacity to surmount adversity. You will encounter this in each narrative presented in these pages. And although this seems an obvious and common character trait, I don't believe that it is. Many people seem to become locked into states of victimhood, directing blame rather than moving past barricades. The mind can obsess upon blame, like a scapegoat to avoid acknowledging resentments and insecurities, or shame, or guilt, or any number of emotions that can be damaging to one's sense-of-self. Yet there is no healing where there is no responsibility. It is easier to be angry than to acknowledge a weakness or flaw.

If this emotion – anger, resentment, blame – could only be harnessed, it could be reshaped into the very trait every medical student in my first-year class possesses. For although it is only subtly different, it is profound: *Grit.*

Yes, it is unfair that some minds can structure chaos while others are dragged into the turbulence of various behavioral health disorders. Similar to any disease, or somatic dysfunction, a behavioral health disorder must first be recognized, and then accepted, and finally treated.

It is a *disorder* only in as much as it traps the mind, and thus the individual.

Each of the medical students in these pages has struggled, and yet they persist. As one's tendency to admit defeat is a character trait, so too is perseverance. How much control do we actually possess over these traits? Perhaps self-efficacy depends on the mind's balance. We have some measure of control over the mind when we recognize and embrace our behavioral health, and if we are not afraid of it, or what it means to be diagnosed with a *disorder*.

There still exists a stigma to being diagnosed with a behavioral health disorder. Fortunately, this antiquated mindset is changing. It is changing because a new generation is recognizing mental health as a component of holistic health care. We are finally trending away from the years of shame and concealment and entering into an era of behavioral health empowerment.

# FIRST YEAR MEDICAL STUDENTS

# LOGAN

*Everyone has mental health challenges – I think it's easiest if we simply talk to each other about our challenges. We might realize that we're a lot more alike than we really think.*

## *Bipolar Disorder*

I STARTED MEDICAL SCHOOL four months ago, and it has been such a fun, wild, and exhilarating journey – from dropping a career in insurance, going back to community college, moving back and forth across the country – *back in with my parents!* – and then moving across the country again, all the way out here to Washington State, and starting my first year of medical school. Maybe you're just a *regular* person – whatever the hell that is – but when I speak of 'mental health,' I'm not necessarily referring to a person who has a diagnosis like I do. What I'm referring to is a person who deals with some sort of mental health challenge in their life. Most of us do.

\* \* \*

I grew up in good old Litchfield, Connecticut, and I didn't have too many mental health challenges growing up. I have a really great family. It's one of the most surprising things to people when I tell them that I have a mental illness. They automatically assume that I must have had a terrible upbringing – but it's really quite the opposite. I had all the opportunities a kid could hope for. My parents would take me skiing. I played sports. My dad would watch nearly all of my sporting events. My mom dropped a career in fashion and went back to school to become an art teacher; eventually she was an art teacher in my school, so I always saw her. We were a really great family, and I'm extremely grateful for that.

My mental health symptoms didn't start until I was in college. I moved to Scotland to study abroad for a year. It was also the first time in my life that I was away from home, in a totally new culture, three-thousand miles from my family and most of my friends – and I don't know if it was from the jetlag or the excitement, but as soon as I got to Scotland, I suddenly couldn't sleep. At first, I just kind of shrugged it off. *It'll go away.* I was sleeping maybe two or three hours a night. But when the second week rolled around, I started to get concerned.

I might have been taking advantage of the fact that the drinking age in Scotland is a bit friendlier than in the United States. I was finally able to buy a pint like a *real* man, so I was having a blast going to all these different bars. I began using alcohol as a sleeping aid. Frankly, I thought the insomnia[1] would go away, so I kept ignoring it. It persisted for a good month. I was starting to feel really exhausted, really irritable, and then I started having an obsessive thought: *Am I going to sleep tonight? Man, I hope I sleep tonight. Oh God, I really need to sleep tonight.* It was terrible, and because I was getting so little sleep, my anxiety was becoming worse. I remember lying in bed and just staring at the clock, thinking to myself: *All right, if I fall asleep at this exact moment, I'll get five hours sleep.* And of course that wouldn't happen. *Okay, if I fall asleep now, I can still get four-and-a-half hours sleep.* It was just a terrible way to live.

The insomnia and anxiety slowly evolved into depression. I was just so exhausted. I would try to go to my dorm room and nap whenever I could, so I was always isolating myself – and that is a weird behavior

---

[1] Insomnia is a common sleep disorder involving trouble falling asleep, staying asleep, or both. As a result, individuals have too little sleep or poor sleep quality, typically waking up not feeling refreshed. Insomnia can be acute (short-term) or chronic (ongoing).

for me, because I'm a very social person. I like being around people. But I wanted to sleep so damn bad that I would isolate myself. The depression started to come on, really come on, about two months into my Scotland experience. I didn't feel like myself. I was barely exercising. I was gaining weight. I was still using alcohol as a sleep aid. And I was in a long-distance relationship at that time. It was extremely challenging.

Fast forward three months – the insomnia was ongoing. Then the depression hit a new craze. I suddenly became convinced that everyone around me hated me. I thought that my parents and sister hated me. I didn't know who I was anymore. It was one of the lowest times of my life. I can remember lying in bed just sulking, and I didn't know why. I could momentarily pull myself out of it by playing basketball, or golfing, or drinking – but as soon as I got back into my isolation, the depression would take over everything in my life.

Saint Andrews is located on these beautiful cliffs. I remember there was a classmate of mine who fell off a cliff and died. Nobody knew if it was a drunken accident, or a suicide, and I was in such a deep state of depression that I remember thinking to myself that I could do that too. It would look like an accident.

These fleeting thoughts would pass and I remember thinking to myself, *No, you don't want to do that, Logan; why would you ever want to do that?* But that thought would return in a week, or in a day, or sometimes just an hour later. What made it worse was that I didn't tell anybody. I never sought a mental health counselor or psychiatrist. I didn't tell my family, or my girlfriend, or any of my friends. I just kept it all to myself.

When I returned to the States, things seemed to get better for a while. But then I started to become irritable; I began having trouble controlling my anger. I still had that gut feeling that everyone hated me. I began to see myself as a loser, just a tool, all the time. But I didn't want anyone to know I was feeling this way. I masked it. I pretended everything was fine. I wanted to come off as the cool kid.

My senior year of college, things were going a little better. My moods were still up and down, but when I was around my friends I could pull out of the depression and have a good time. As soon as I was isolated again, the depression would come back. Then, around the time that I graduated, I went through a tough breakup. It was the first serious relationship of my life. And I was transitioning away from being a full-time student and entering into the 'real world.' I had a job lined up as an underwriter at an insurance group in Worcester, Massachusetts. I was really nervous about it. I didn't know if I would be happy working in insurance – but when they told me what my salary would be, it was like, okay, yea that's cool, let's do *that*. I'm embarrassed to say it now, but at that time of my life I believed money would make me happy.

Graduation week rolled around, the breakup had happened, and all of a sudden I was euphoric. I had just finished four years at Holy Cross[2]. I was about to graduate with an economics degree. I was partying. It was a great time. And the euphoria I was experiencing fit in with what everyone around me was feeling. All my classmates were partying. It was incredible. However, it was then that the insomnia returned with full force. The week after my girlfriend and I broke up, it became insane – the true extreme of insomnia. Absolutely zero sleep. And it continued right through graduation week.

On about day three, things began to get weird. I started having racing thoughts. It was like conversations

---

[2] College of the Holy Cross is four-year liberal arts undergraduate college in Worcester, Massachusetts. It was founded in 1843 by Jesuits, and currently has roughly 3,000 students.

taking place in my head. People around me couldn't understand what I was trying to say. I was sort of spitting out random words and thoughts. I felt this desire to let people know that I had been depressed but I'm better now. I think this is when my friends and family started to notice that something was off. But how do you intervene? I began having grandiose thoughts. I thought I would start a website about mental health. I planned it all out in my head. My brain was working super-fast. I thought I was a genius.

It was a manic episode[3] straight out of a textbook.

By about day four, I was having thoughts of starting a non-profit website that would save the mental health world. Then I began essentially harassing the parents of my classmates. I wanted them to invest in my idea. I thought I was the next Mark Zuckerberg[4], or Elon Musk[5]. I just needed some money to get started. I

---

[3] A manic episode is a symptom of bipolar disorder, type 1. These episodes are typically described as feeling elated, full of energy, difficulty sleeping, irritable, racing thoughts, sense of grandiosity, and engaging in risk-taking behaviors. Manic episodes normally require immediate hospital care, and are followed by a depressed episode.

[4] Mark Zuckerberg is the Cofounder, Chairman, and CEO of Facebook. As of April 2, 2019, he has an estimated net worth of $64.8 billion. Zuckerberg started Facebook at Harvard University in 2004, at the age of 19, and took the company public in May 2012.

[5] Elon Musk is the CEO and Chairman of Tesla. Musk founded Tesla

don't think my family or friends knew how to react. It was probably scary for them. Something was clearly happening with me. I remember people approaching me and asking, 'Are you okay? What's going on? Are you on cocaine or something?' And I was like, 'No, what are you talking about? Get away from me.'

By day five, I thought the FBI was following me. I was driving around all day with a deep paranoia. I thought people were listening to my thoughts, going through my phone, hacking into my computer. Then the auditory hallucinations started. I began having conversations with a voice in my head, I don't know who. I thought everything was normal, but it was the people around me who realized that something was wrong. I went to my graduation, and when I came home, there were people waiting for me. My parents had arranged for them. I like to call them The Mental Health Avengers; but really, they were an emergency response team for mental health crisis situations.

'Logan, are you a little off? Can you recognize that you're not acting normally right now?' I was in the midst of a manic episode, but I had the insight to realize that I hadn't slept in five days. Then they laid out to me

---

Motors in 2003 to bring fully-electric vehicles to the mass market. He also owns SpaceX, a rocket company, valued at more than $20 billion.

was that there aren't enough psychiatrists, that there is essentially a wait list, and I might not be able to get help right away. Alternatively, I could go to the emergency room. I would see the hospital psychiatrist. But I would have to check myself into the Psychiatric Ward.

*What? Are you kidding me? You want to send me to the Psych Ward? What?*

I walked off. I spoke a lot of expletives. And then two of my best friends called me. They were really the influencers who helped motivate me. They told me they loved me, but the only way they could see me getting better was by getting help as soon as possible. I couldn't ignore this. I was about to start a job. I *had* to go.

And so I did. I showed up to a hospital in Torrington, Connecticut. *How the hell did I end up here?* You see, when you show up at the emergency room and you're in a state of psychosis, they don't put you next to the kid who broke his arm. There's a big room with massive doors and locks. It reminded me of an industrial refrigerator. A security guard was standing out front. *What's going to happen?* They took me to a room with a bed that had attached belts to secure your head and chest and stirrups for your feet. *Are you kidding me?* 'You better not strap me to that bed.'

'Sir, we won't. Just stay calm. You're going to get through this.'

I didn't stay in that refrigerator-room for too long. They moved me into the Psych Ward. For the most part, it wasn't too bad. I do remember occasionally hearing people screaming throughout the night. There were group therapy sessions throughout the day that I would attend. And I did get to meet with a psychiatrist. I don't want to paint this as a pretty picture. All I wanted to do was get out of there. I would just pace the halls and stare out the windows. 'Can I go on a walk at least?' – 'Uh, no sir.' They would take me to this little sun room on the top floor of the hospital, fully enclosed of course, so there was hardly any fresh air. I remember feeling just terrible.

*How the hell did I end up here? And now you're telling me I have bipolar disorder? What?*

In the group therapy sessions, they would warn us about the mental health stigma. It's a real thing. You can't be ignorant to it. It can jeopardize your career. People might not want to be in a relationship with you. Don't wear this like a badge of pride. People might judge you. I remember thinking – *Yea, but they might not. People might be okay with it. What's the big deal?* I kind of tuned off at that point. *Whatever. You don't have bipolar disorder, I do. Just shut up.*

I'll never forget those five days I spent in the Psych Ward. It was an extremely difficult time for me. When you finally get out, you think it's going to be so much easier now. *I'm finally out of this damn place.* But it's not easier. You get out, sure, but at least in the Psych Ward you're surrounded by people who are like you, people who have a mental illness. All of a sudden you're out and who can you talk to about this? I felt so alone. I felt more alone than when I was in Scotland. I had just been through the Psychiatric Ward. I was prescribed *Abilify*[6]. I actually ended up having a weird side effect from the drug where I was always twitching my leg; I learned later that it might become permanent if I hadn't switched to a new antipsychotic. But I didn't

---

[6] Brand: Abilify, Generic: Aripiprazole. Among antipsychotics, aripiprazole uniquely acts as a partial D2 agonist; at increased concentrations, typical in elders, more complete dopaminergic inhibition results. Aripiprazole is associated with an elevated risk of akathisia (intense subjective feeling of restlessness), sedation, nausea, headache, weight gain, and increased cholesterol levels.

have anyone to talk to. No one around me knew what it was like to be taking *Abilify*.

I started working at an insurance group. I hated my job. It paid well, but I was in a cubicle working on spreadsheets all day long. I was underwriting – analyzing risk of inland and marina insurance and earthquakes … it was so boring! I stared at the walls all day. I felt so depressed. I just stayed at home, never exercising, gaining all this weight. And then I was transferred. It was the best thing about the job. They sent me to Sacramento, California. I was still adjusting from the breakup with the ex-girlfriend, and learning to live with bipolar disorder, and I remember thinking that, okay, here's a new chance. I'm going to move to California. And, you know what, I'm tired of being embarrassed of my mental illness. This is a garbage way to live. Statistics tell me that there are a lot of people with bipolar out there, and even more with depression. This is an opportunity. I can start talking about this. Prior to that, I hadn't even talked to my best friends about the Psych Ward. I was embarrassed. But I wouldn't know anybody in California. I moved in with a couple guys I met online, and I figured I would just tell them; if they thought I was crazy, I'd just move out. Once I started talking about my mental illness, people encouraged me to find others. There have to be others like me out there.

I found a bipolar and depression support group called *Balanced*[7]. It took me six months before I had the guts to show up, but it was one of the best things I ever did. We met every Wednesday night in a little old church in downtown Sacramento. I met people who had been living with bipolar disorder for twenty years. It was the first time I sat down with people who knew what I went through. I felt so inspired. These people are living normal and great lives. But I found it odd that they didn't speak out about their mental health. That's when I really started to learn about the mental health stigma. I heard stories of rough breakups, people losing their jobs. It was everything the mental health professionals had warned me about. But the world isn't going to change unless people start speaking out.

I was still dealing with bipolar symptoms pretty severely: depression, bits of insomnia, and I was really frustrated. I felt lackadaisical. Eventually my medication was changed for a fourth time and I was started on *Depakote*[8]. But I was still embarrassed about

---

[7] *Balanced* is a weekly, in-person support group based out of Sacramento, California, for anyone affected by mood disorders who want practical tools to improve their quality of life. More information can be found at www.meetup.com/Balanced/

my bipolar disorder. Outside of that *Balanced* community, I didn't talk about it all that much. Many of my friends didn't know the specifics of what I had gone through – maybe they had heard some things, but not from me. I was still dragging myself out of bed every morning to go stare at the walls of my cubicle. I was just lugging. Then one day, I got on the scale; I weighed two-hundred-seventy-five pounds. I felt disgusting. People would tell me about the power of exercise, and so I decided to take it seriously. I started working out, and of course I did start to lose weight – but more importantly, my mental health began to improve. I began feeling less irritable. I was sleeping better, feeling less anxious.

And then came a day I'll never forget. It was December 14, 2012, the day of the Sandy Hook Shooting[9]. My mom was an elementary school art teacher in my hometown of Litchfield, Connecticut, about an hour north of Sandy Hook, and so it hit really close to home for me. All day long the news was

---

[8] Depakote is the brand name for the generic medication, Valproic Acid. This medication was originally used to treat certain types of seizures, but has been found to be beneficial for bipolar disorder, as well as in preventing migraine headaches.

[9] The Sandy Hook Elementary School shooting occurred on December 14, 2012 in Newtown, Connecticut. It left 28 people dead and 2 injured. After murdering his mother at their home, Adam Lanza fatally shot 20 children and 6 adults at the elementary school before taking his own life.

commenting on how people with mental health issues can't be controlled. They shouldn't have access to guns. They're inherently violent. The media was portraying the story in such a light. It changed my attitude about a lot of things. Sure, some people with mental illness might be violent – but not *everybody*. I could never commit the atrocities that were committed that day. And I am one of those people with a mental illness. I remember feeling that I needed to do something, because people will continue to make unfair assumptions unless we speak out and do something. If we're not active in trying to change this unfair misconception, people who need help won't seek the treatment they need.

A friend of mine who worked with Mental Health America[10] had asked me if I would speak at a bureau addressing mental health disorders in the community. I hadn't felt comfortable speaking in public then. I wasn't ready. I was too nervous. Maybe someday, sure, when I have a better job, or a better house, or when I'm married ... then I'll be ready, but not yet. Then Sandy Hook happened, and I called my friend, and I told him it was time. I went through the

---

[10] Mental Health America is a nonprofit dedicated to addressing the needs of those living with mental illness and to promote the overall mental health of all Americans. The organization was founded in 1909; it has 200 affiliates, 6,500 affiliate staff, and over 10,000 volunteers across 41 states.

training. And I realized that I had a knack for public speaking. I went to universities and told my story. I went to hospitals. I spoke to police officers. I began to feel that I was finally doing something proactive. I enjoyed it. It began to feel almost hypomanic[11].

Hypomania. It's not quite a full-blown manic episode like what I experienced during the week of my college graduation. It's the pre-stage to that. You feel energized. You feel really good. You crash hard when it passes, and you might feel drained, and depressed. It's different for everyone. How often you experience these hypomanic episodes, how long they might last, how hard you finally crash when they pass. I began to feel hypomanic about mental health. To be honest, it felt quite similar to the manic episode I had experienced before, yet it was different. I was medicated now. I was on the *Depakote*. I was seeing a therapist regularly. I had control over the energy I was feeling.

I was struck with the idea of posting my story on *YouTube* because I thought it was unfair to my friends that they didn't know the details of what I had been through. I was going to schools and hospitals and

---

[11] Hypomania is described as a mood state that is elevated above normal, but not so extreme as to cause impairment, which distinguishes it from mania. Similar to mania, hypomanic episodes require less sleep and reported increases in energy.

getting paid for giving these public speeches about my bipolar disorder, but some of my best friends didn't know the whole story. I wasn't okay with that. So one night I was just sitting in my kitchen in front of my computer and I started recording what the past three years of my life had been like. It was a wild journey. Depressed in Scotland. Struggling with thoughts of suicide. Entering the Psych Ward. Gaining weight and losing weight and becoming a public speaker and now sitting in front of my computer in my kitchen telling my story. I posted it online. I was immediately terrified. Is my job going to be cool with this? Will any girl ever want to date me when she searches my name on Google? (because let's be real, ladies, we know you do.) But I rolled the dice. And then that post on *YouTube* changed my life.

Within a few hours, the video had a thousand hits. People were sharing it. It started to go mini-viral. Within a week, it had ten-thousand views. By the end of the month, it had thirty-thousand views. If you see it now, you'll see a twenty-three-year-old Logan just going for it, not knowing what else to do, just wanting to contribute *something* to the mental health community. I had no idea I would become a doctor then. I just knew that I was frustrated with the mental health system. Then I was invited for an interview on

*Foxnews.com*[12], about why I posted a video about my bipolar disorder, and about how the video was helping people confront their own mental health. People were reaching out to me. Everybody had an experience that they had been through; maybe they had bipolar disorder, maybe it was in their family, maybe it was another mental health challenge. I was talking to old friends of mine about mental health, and to people I had never met before. I wanted to be a part of the mental health community, but I still felt so lost. I wanted to find my place in all of it.

    I decided to create a group similar to the bipolar and depression group *Balanced*, but with a focus on physical fitness. When your physical health is nurtured, your mental health will follow. I called it *Blissify*. It was a mental health fitness group. I put flyers up all around the *Balanced* support group, and maybe fourteen people showed up. I was so excited. And then what happened? I ran! I had a whistle. We did a hard workout. Now I was in the best shape of my life back then. I was running all the time. What I hadn't accounted for was that most of the people who showed

---

[12] Logan was featured on FoxNews.com on March 7, 2013 by Loren Grush, in an episode entitled "No Longer Silent: Man With Bipolar Disorder Speaks Up About His Illness, Inspiring Others." The article can be accessed by searching the article title, or searching 'Logan Noone' via simple internet search.

up to *Blissify* weren't in good shape, which is why they were showing up in the first place. Most of them were dealing with depression, and this was an early effort to try to start working out. The second week, only three people showed up. I realized that I needed to modify *Blissify*. It eventually turned into a walking group; sometimes we would go swimming, biking, or hiking, but mostly we walked around McKinley Park in Sacramento.

When I turned twenty-four, I was invited to be the key note speaker at the 2013 National Alliance on Mental Illness Walk[13] in Sacramento. It was in front of about fifteen-hundred people. I gave perhaps the most passionate speech I've ever given. I met a State Senator who went on to become the mayor of Sacramento. Then I was invited to throw the first pitch at a Sacramento River Cats game for Mental Health Matters Day[14]. The next thing I knew I was recording a public service announcement on behalf of Mental Health America that was broadcast throughout California in an effort to bring mental health awareness into the mainstream.

---

[13] National Alliance on Mental Illness, NAMI, is a grassroots mental health organization dedicated to building better lives for millions of Americans affected by mental illness. The group was founded by families in 1979. The organization offers education and advocacy for individuals living with mental illness.

[14] Mental Health Matters Day is organized through Mental Health America of California. The event hosts speakers, entertainers, exhibits and sponsors to honor and celebrate mental health recovery.

And all throughout this time, I was still working in insurance.

I changed jobs within the same insurance group. I had been working as a risk analyst for two years, and then I moved into sales, which I thought would be better – but actually it was worse. I had to make eighty cold sales calls a day. 'Hello sir, have you looked at any different insurance options, especially your worker's compensation; I know you're an electrical contractor, and that can be quite expensive; would you ever like to take a look at ... – eighty of *those* a day: leaving voicemails, going to networking meetings, trying to kiss the asses of business owners so that they might look at different insurance options, so they can save money, so we can earn money. It was so boring. And I knew that I needed to be involved in mental health – I just didn't know what to do.

I thought maybe I could turn *Blissify* into a non-profit organization. And then I thought maybe I could become a therapist. But what I *really* dreamed of was becoming a psychiatrist. But it wasn't realistic. I had an economics degree. I considered going into nursing and focusing on psychiatric health, but I just wasn't sure. I wanted to contribute to the understanding of mental health. I wanted to help catch people earlier in their diagnoses, so that we can avoid the unnecessary suicides related to mental illness[15]. I strongly believed, and I still do, that there is a genetic component to mental illness. My uncle had bipolar disorder. He committed suicide. My cousin has been diagnosed. We suspect that my grandmother was probably bipolar.

I met a guy in Sacramento who had taken all the premedical requirements but wasn't sure if he wanted to go into medicine. He wasn't sure if the path was worth the effort. Like me, he was making decent money, but he just didn't like his job. He was working as a health care consultant. But what he taught me was that the dream of medical school isn't as farfetched as you might think. There are lots of people who go back to school to take the premedical requirements and the med school entrance exam. I realized that, yes, I do want to go back to school. I want to study medicine. I want to focus on the science. I want to learn the genetics of mental illness so that we can save more lives.

To be honest, I didn't think I was smart enough for medical school.

---

[15] Suicide is the 10th leading cause of death in the United States for all ages. Every day, approximately 123 Americans die by suicide – one every 12 minutes.

I started to talk about it. I began telling people that I was going to be a mental health professional. Then I left the world of insurance and moved in with my girlfriend in Yuba City, California. I enrolled at a community college, and I'll never forget that first semester. I was taking general chemistry, biology, and Spanish. I was twenty-five years old, sitting next to all these kids fresh out of high school – eighteen years old, braces on their teeth, super awkward around each other – and I was so excited to be there. I was motivated because I was paying for it all myself, and I did really well academically. I began to think that maybe I *could* actually get into medical school.

After two semesters, I was all in. Those years were an interesting time in my life. I began working as a driving instructor because I could schedule work around my classes. Then I got a job at a local mental health facility right there in Yuba City. I was feeling really good about myself, but I became so focused on school and working to pay for school that I began to let my mental health slip. All the good habits I had learned became secondary. I wasn't working out. I started putting on weight. I had less energy. I became more irritable. My girlfriend and I were fighting all the time. I was finally pursuing a path in life that I was excited about, but I noticed these changes in my moods.

If you don't know this, applying to medical school is incredibly expensive. First you have to take all the prerequisite coursework, and even though I went to a community college, it still adds up. You have to pay about four-hundred dollars to take the MCAT[16]. You have to pay for preparation materials. Some students take a preparatory class. Then you have to pony out about one-hundred dollars per application. Most applicants apply to about twenty schools. Then you fork out another hundred-dollars for each supplemental application, which includes a second batch of essays specific for every school. So all of a sudden you have all this work to do, because most schools send you a secondary application pretty quickly after you submit your primary application. Some medical schools will waive application fees, but I didn't meet those requirements. Then you have to travel around the country to all these different schools if they choose to interview you. It's one fee on top of another. I realized it was going to cost me anywhere between four-thousand and seven-thousand dollars just to apply, and only about one in ten students who apply are actually

---

[16] The Medical College Admission Test (MCAT) is developed and administered by the AAMC, Association of American Medical Colleges. This is a standardized, multiple-choice examination created to help medical school admissions assess problem solving, critical thinking, and knowledge of natural, behavioral, and social science.

offered a seat. I didn't know how I was going to do it financially.

'Hey, baby, I think I'm going to need to move back in with my parents.'

I knew she was a keeper when she agreed to move three-thousand miles from California to Connecticut to move in with my parents so that I could chase my dream of medical school. Three months later, I asked her to marry me. My beautiful Migdelina. Yes, we're married. She's awesome.

Back in good old Litchfield, Connecticut – living with my parents, my fiancée, and our two cats – I found a job at an addiction center. I was working in an all-male halfway home. It really taught me what addiction is, because nobody starts taking drugs with the intention of becoming an addict. I would hear these stories that, to be honest, didn't sound all that different from my own story. Just normal guys. After they completed four-to-six weeks of in-treatment, and now completely off drugs, in *my* house, they're allowed back into the community. They would work right down the street at a restaurant that the treatment facility owned. If they were eligible, they could have their own car. It was great seeing these guys integrate back into society. Addiction can happen to anybody. Maybe it's the result of mental illness, or trauma, or maybe a social situation triggers a person into a coping mechanism that isn't necessarily the healthiest.

During the medical school application process, I was working at the treatment facility. After you submit all your applications, then you just wait. I used to check my email a gross number of times every day, just hoping for an offer to interview at a school. I was fortunate. I ended up with five interviews. I was waitlisted at two schools. And then, a day I'll never forget – I had taken the guys from the house to a paintball course, and then I got the phone call. I was offered a seat. All the way out in the Pacific Northwest. We all started hollering and shooting our paintball guns into the air.

Medical school has evoked from me a whole spectrum of emotions. I have been so excited, so happy to be here. At the same time, it is absurdly challenging. I knew that it would be an incredible amount of work, the hardest thing I've ever done, but it's even harder than that. And yet, because of the mental health challenges I've experienced in my life, I've brought a lot of lessons and strategies with me, and I've been active in using them. I try to keep myself balanced through the stresses of medical school.

I got in. I'm in medical school. So many people told me throughout the application process that I shouldn't mention my bipolar disorder. It's a bad idea. It's not going to strengthen your application. But I didn't want to live that kind of life. It's important to me that people talk out about mental illness. I don't want to sacrifice that. We have to eradicate the stigma surrounding mental health. More people can be saved if they are willing to use the mental health system, because in my eyes, it seems that when people finally crash, or peek, or attempt suicide – or, in my case, enter a psychosis – that's often the first time they meet with a mental health professional. We need to change this.

Talking about my mental illness is my driving force, and yet all of the advice I kept hearing was that I shouldn't alert medical schools to the fact that I have any sort of disability. It's going to make you into a red flag. Medical school is already hard enough to get into. I didn't follow that advice. I didn't want to start my medical career by hiding the reason I wanted to go into medicine in the first place. So I decided to be open about it. I even wrote about it in my application essays. When I submitted those applications, I remember feeling sick to my stomach – just like I did after I posted that very first *YouTube* video. Did I just throw everything away? Did I just waste years of effort and all of my money by admitting that I have bipolar disorder?

In the back of my mind, there was one more *YouTube* video that I wanted to make. And I finally did. I posted it during my first week as a medical student. I was nervous. Are the students in my class going to think I'm just some weirdo? Of course, they didn't. In fact, they were excited that I was so open about it, and that I was in school with them. It gave me the opportunity to talk with many of them about their own mental health, because many of us are dealing with mental health issues. I was told not to talk about these things because it would jeopardize my career. It would keep me from being accepted. But here I am. *I made it!* I didn't listen to them. I lived my life on my own terms. Yes, I have a mental illness, but it's not all of me. It's a part of me. And I'm not ashamed of it.

# MEGAN

*I consciously know that what I'm thinking is irrational, but I feel an absolute need to carry out the compulsion. It's like, I know this a dumb thought that has nothing to do with the situation, but it feels like it has so much meaning behind it, and I wish it didn't.*

***Obsessive Compulsive Disorder***
***Attention Deficit Hyperactivity Disorder***

IT'S IMPORTANT we recognize that this is normal. People go through these things, and it's healthy that we talk about it. Having a mental health disorder is a disease, like having diabetes. It's something that people suffer from that affects their day-to-day life. I'm twenty-seven years old now, a first-year medical student, and I was *diagnosed*-diagnosed when I was nineteen – but my parents think I've had OCD[17] symptoms since forever.

I remember the moment when it all kind of started –

---

[17] Obsessive-Compulsive Disorder (OCD) – features include irrational ideas or impulses that persistently intrude into awareness. Patients often experience obsessions, anxiety provoking thoughts, compulsions, and repetitive actions. The prevalence in the general population is 2-3%.

I was eleven. My friend's mom had driven me home from softball practice. She died the next day. She was the first person I knew who died. It was a random, accidental death. Suddenly she was just gone.

Over the years, some therapists have suggested that what I experienced was PTSD – but I think I was predisposed to having a mental health condition and that the death of my friend's mom triggered it. Ever since then, I have been anxious. Eventually my anxiety became ritualistic. If I didn't flick the lights on-and-off four times, then I knew that something bad would happen to my mother. I was particularly anxious about my parents. I remember performing rituals in the bathroom of my middle school. When I was in high school, I remember my parents telling me that I should go to therapy. But I had very particular views about therapy back then, about what might and might not work, and I hadn't accepted that OCD was a part of me. Thinking about it just made me more anxious.

My parents tell me that when I was four or five years old, I began to express a significant amount of concern for family members. And so they began to look into possible etiologies of this characteristic. They discovered something called *PANDAS*: Pediatric Autoimmune Neuropsychiatric Disorders Associated with Streptococcal Infections[18]. It is a theory that links serious childhood strep infections with the development of OCD in later life. When I was even younger, I had had a bad reaction to sulfa medications[19] that had to do with a strep infection, so my parents got the notion that the strep infection I had suffered might be related to my OCD. We have a history in my family of anxiety and depression – but never OCD.

When I was in high school my parents began to take note of my behavior. I remember they took me to a therapist, and I remember the therapist doing CBT[20] with me. The idea with Cognitive Behavioral Therapy,

---

[18] Pediatric autoimmune neuropsychiatric disorders associated with Streptococcus infections (PANDAS) is a neurological and psychiatric condition in which symptoms are brought on or worsened by Streptococcal infection. Symptoms typically appear between 3 years of age and puberty.

[19] Sulfa drugs treat a wide range of health problems, but can sometimes cause allergic reactions in certain patients. Allergies most often occur with antibiotics. Around 3% of people have some type of reaction to these medications. Reactions include skin rash, hives, itching, breathing problems, and swelling, and rarely, fatal Stevens Johnson syndrome.

[20] Cognitive–behavioral therapy (CBT) is an evidence-based therapeutic technique that emphasizes an educational and skill-building approach, stressing collaboration between the therapist and patient in identifying and modifying factors that contribute to emotional disorders or problematic behaviors. Treatment aims to modify the thoughts, feelings, and behaviors causing distress. CBT has substantial empirical support in the treatment of depression, anxiety, eating disorders, substance abuse, and chronic pain conditions. Given the frequent maladaptive thoughts, behaviors, and emotions among rehabilitation patients, CBT is quite applicable to individuals with chronic health conditions and acquired injury.

especially with OCD patients, and probably anybody with anxiety, is to expose the person to the anxiety, and then instead of going and flicking the light switch four times, or whatever you need to do to feel better, you're supposed to sit with the anxiety until eventually it goes away. Or so you hope. The problem was that I wasn't fully aware of what was happening with me. I hadn't accepted that OCD was an issue with me yet, and I didn't have the tools to deal with the anxiety I was feeling if I didn't carry out my compulsions.

I've heard OCD described as the worst form of anxiety. Of course, I don't have anything to compare it to; for me, it's just the anxiety that I feel every day. It's certainly burdensome. Sometimes I even have it in my sleep. I'll be performing OCD rituals in my dreams. I wake up and feel as though I've been anxious all night long, which is terrible, because sleep is supposed to be the time when I'm free from my world of anxiety. I'm supposed to finally recover when I go to sleep.

In college I learned to practice DBT[21]. Dialectical Behavioral Therapy is something I think

---

[21] Dialectical behavior therapy (DBT) is a cognitive-behavioral approach that focuses on behavioral change while providing acceptance, compassion, and validation of the patient. Several randomized trials have demonstrated the efficacy of DBT in the treatment of personality disorders.

everyone could benefit from. It focuses on mindfulness and interpersonal relationships. It taught me to recognize that a thought is only a thought, a momentary thing, and it's okay to be experiencing it. DBT took away the superfluous feelings that accompanied my thoughts, so when I sit with my thoughts and feelings, I can do it without attributing so much meaning to them. It's the meaning that can be so disturbing. This is only a thought and nothing more, and nothing less, and it will pass.

And so the compulsions and obsessions really started after my friend's mom died when I was eleven years old, but when I was nineteen years old and a sophomore in college, things got really bad. I had spent the summer in Panama, working with a volunteer organization, and I spent a lot of time by myself that summer. Now I'm a very social person; being by myself is not my normal. I remember my mom saying how I came back from Panama an entirely different person. I think that summer was another trigger that aggravated my OCD. I was a sophomore in college and I had to drop out of all my classes.

Our family doctor formally diagnosed me – but really it was my parents. They are both physicians. But because it would be ethically inappropriate for them to diagnose their own child, I went to our family doctor. He put me on *Prozac*[22]. When I was younger, my parents didn't want me taking meds or any kind of SSRI[23] because I was still physically developing. But I'm glad I was prescribed the *Prozac* when I was nineteen. It has been really helpful. I like to say that it's a very gentle drug. It definitely doesn't cure my OCD, but it makes me feel more in control of it. I was on *Prozac* for a few years before I weaned myself off of it. I thought I didn't need it anymore. For four or five years I was off of it, until this past summer, before starting first year of medical school, when my anxiety became really bad again. I just didn't know what to expect in medical school. There were two times this summer when I felt least stressed. The first was when I climbed Mount Rainier with my brother. A misstep could be devastating and so I was completely focused on what I was doing. The second was when I was fly-fishing with my dad. It was just so calming being outside and hearing the water and focusing on that little

---

[22] *Prozac (Trade name): Fluoxetine (Generic).* Fluoxetine was the first SSRI to become available on the market in 1988. This drug ushered in a new era of treatment, providing an alternative to the TCAs (tricyclic antidepressants). In geriatric patients, fluoxetine has demonstrated superiority as compared to placebo, and is as efficacious as amitriptyline, doxepin, escitalopram, paroxetine, sertraline, and trimipramine.

[23] SSRI: selective serotonin receptor inhibitor. The acute effect of SSRIs is a highly selective action on the serotonin transporter (SERT). SSRIs allosterically inhibit the transporter, binding at a site other than that of serotonin. They have minimal inhibitory effects on the norepinephrine transporter or blocking actions on adrenergic and cholinergic receptors.

fly drifting on the surface. I think both of those experiences forced my mind to stay in the moment.

There are different categories of OCD. There is the classic kind where a person is compelled to wash their hands obsessively. You might notice a person's hands are all chapped. I don't have that problem. I'm kind of the opposite. I'm very messy. Then there are people who are super religious and feel they have to recite specific prayers a certain number of times. And then there's trichotillomania[24], obsessively pulling out your hair. Even hoarding[25] is said to be a form of OCD.

With my OCD, the obsessions are always the same. My obsessions concern bad things happening to people I love if I don't do certain things. I have a hard time reading newspapers because I internalize the tragedies that I read about; and I have a hard time watching movies or shows when I know a character is going to die. It's not that I'm sympathize for the person

---

[24] Trichotillomania is hair loss caused by damage to the hair follicle by constant pulling or tension over a long period, related to a compulsive disorder. This behavior results in bizarre patterns of hair loss. The prevalence is estimated to be 1.5% of males and 3.4% of females in the United States.

[25] Hoarding is observed in many syndromes other than OCD, including anorexia nervosa, Tourette syndrome, autism, stimulant abuse, and others. These patients have hidden stashes of items that they have collected. These items often have little tangible importance to the individual.

who dies – it's that I empathize for the people who have to cope with the loss. These are my *obsessions*. My *compulsions*, however, have changed over the years. When I was younger, I would flick the lights on and off all the time. Even numbers are better than odd numbers. I can't tell you why. I'd flick lights four times, or eight times. I remember in college walking in and out of my friend's dorm room four times, and she said, 'Oh, a little OCD, are we?'

'Actually, yes.'

She felt pretty bad, but then we talked about it and she really helped me, and she still helps me. What happens is that I consciously know that what I'm thinking is irrational, but I feel an absolute need to carry out the compulsion. It's like, I *know* this a dumb thought that has nothing to do with the situation, but it *feels* like it has so much meaning behind it, and I wish it didn't.

So – fun fact – I also have ADHD[26]. I was diagnosed this year, so I'm pretty excited about that. Having ADHD and OCD is an interesting mix. They

---

[26] Attention-deficit/hyperactivity disorder (ADHD) is a brain disorder marked by an ongoing pattern of inattention and/or hyperactivity-impulsivity that interferes with functioning or development.

both fall under the big umbrella of Anxiety, but when my OCD makes me obsessed over one thought, my ADHD turns me into a squirrel bouncing from one thought to another.

I don't currently see a therapist. I think I've learned to become a lot better at recognizing when I need to prioritize *me*, and when I have to prioritize my mental health over my school work. I know that if I don't take care of myself, then I won't be able to focus, and then I won't be able to accomplish the things that I need to get done. And so sometimes I have to just hang out with a friend, or call my mom, or go outside for a while. These things are really helpful for me. And I've become better at coping with failure. I've become a lot better at being comfortable with things being uncomfortable – because I've been in that stage of my life where I had no hope. I was only able to pull myself out with help from my family and friends. I didn't do it by myself. And it's terrible to feel so low. When you finally come out of that low, you can look back and use that time as comparison. It's not as bad now as it once was, and I survived that, so this too will pass.

That sophomore year of college when I was really sick, one very positive thing that came from it was that I gained the tools to help me manage my OCD.

Today, as a medical student, I realize that my extremely busy schedule is actually quite helpful. My OCD is still with me, of course, but I'm better at saying to myself, *All right, Megan, you need to focus on what's in front of you right now.* I have to reassure myself that my thoughts don't make me who I am. Because I'm thinking something doesn't make it real. It's still only a thought. I like to think that I'm *neutralizing* the thought. And so rather than giving it a negative association, I acknowledge that it's a thought, only a thought, and then I can move on.

I have a tendency to make assumptions about people. If I see a person eating alone at a restaurant, for instance, I might assume loneliness – and that's not a fair assumption. Sometimes people like to be by themselves. So it's an unreasonable thought. I have to neutralize that thought and not let myself get ensnared in it. When I'm feeling anxious, or even if I'm feeling in a bit of a rut, I try to sit back and just watch – and recognize that it's going to be rough sometimes, and then it's going to get better.

There's a series of books called The Adolescent Mental Health Initiative[27]. They're written about

---

[27] "Treating and Preventing Adolescent Mental Health Disorders: What We Know and What We Don't Know," is an overview of adolescent

particular mental health disorders by people with those very disorders. I read a book called *The Thought That Counts*[28] about a young guy with OCD. I realized that I had thoughts exactly like the character, and I just didn't know how to verbalize them. But this book captured how it felt to have OCD. Because it can be difficult for someone to understand it if they've never experienced it, I started giving the book to family and friends. Maybe they might have a better understanding of what life was like for me.

I applied to the Peace Corps after college, but I was afraid that I wasn't going to be accepted because of my mental health. I was seeing a counselor at the time, and she had to submit a form declaring that I was basically mentally stable enough to participate. I remember she called me and asked what accommodations I would need abroad. I told her I was up for anything. But it was a powerful moment for me – that she trusted me to make my own call about where I

---

mental health disorders that was updated in 2017, and available online as free e-book. The book examines various groups including anxiety disorders, schizophrenia, depression, bipolar disorder, eating disorders, substance and alcohol abuse, and suicide prevention.

[28] *The Thought That Counts:* For the more than two million Americans with obsessive-compulsive disorder, the intrusive thoughts and uncontrollable behaviors can take a harsh toll, as author Jared Douglas Kant knows all too well. Diagnosed with OCD at age 11, Jared became ruled by dread of deadly germs and diseases, the unrelenting need to count and check things, and a persistent, nagging doubt that overshadowed his life.

was mentally and emotionally. I felt really grateful to her. I remember her telling me how she had been rejected from the Peace Corps when she was my age because of an eating disorder she had been diagnosed with as an adolescent that was considered a mental health problem. I spent my Peace Corps tour in Guatemala. A lot of the volunteers had difficult times. Some of my friends had to early-terminate because of mental health issues. But I was fortunate, and my mental health was okay those years that I was abroad. I go through ebbs and flows in my life. Certain years are better than others and my Peace Corps were good.

When I started medical school – and I know that it was challenging for everybody – but I had to figure out how my OCD and ADHD were going to impact me as a student. I'm still trying to figure it out actually. Part of me is afraid that if I take a stimulant it might influence my OCD, so I haven't taken *Adderall*[29] or anything for my ADHD. It would be great if it helped me to better focus on studying, but if it were to heighten my focus on obtrusive thoughts, then that could be a major detriment. I might test medications this summer. I might start on a very gentle dose of *Ritalin*[30]. But I

---

[29] Adderall: generic: Amphetamine Salt Combo. Duration 4-6 hours, short acting stimulant, dextroamphetamine family.
[30] Ritalin: generic: Methylphenidate. Duration 4-6 hours, short acting stimulant, methyl family.

just don't know. I'm doing okay in school right now, much better than first semester, but I'm still working on learning how to handle everything. It's kind of a daily – not struggle – but effort.

It takes a lot mental energy to go to a therapist and work on your emotional health, and it takes a lot of time. To really try and beat this OCD I think I need to do what they call *Exposure and Response Therapy*[31]. You see, I want to be a really good doctor, and one thing I'm afraid of, about becoming a doctor, is having to tell families that their loved one has died, or that their loved one has terminal cancer, or having to tell someone that *they* have terminal cancer. I think I'll be good at it, because I'm very empathetic and compassionate, but I'm afraid it's something that I'll take home with me. This is a fear that I obsess over.

I've thought a lot about different medical specialties that might suite me. I once worked in an Emergency Room, and what's good about the ER when you have OCD and ADHD is that you move from

---

[31] Exposure and response prevention therapy (ERPT) helps you deal with your anxiety and fears by exposing you to something that upsets you and then helping you practice new ways of responding. Over time, you are able to stay relaxed when you are exposed to something that used to upset you. Trained mental health specialists provide this type of therapy. ERPT often takes 10 to 20 or more sessions to be effective.

patient to patient very quickly. If a patient dies, yes, you tell the family – but then you immediately move to the next patient. This might be good for me. You don't really get to know your patients all too well, but the downside is that it's your responsibility to inform families of the status of loved ones. Alternatively, in a specialization like family medicine, you become deeply involved in your patients' lives. Your patients essentially become a part of your life. So it will hurt when a patient dies, but at least you probably won't be there *when* they die.

It was in the early months of first year medical school that I asked myself: *Is it normal for me to be so off the walls incapable of paying attention?* And I took the ADHD test that the school offers. There are multiple ADHD tests out there. We went into a room and I sat in front of the computer. The program looked like it was from the 1970's, a green and black screen, very janky. The first part of the test, when I saw the number 1, I had to click the mouse. When I saw the number 2, I did not click the mouse. Then the numbers start flashing: 1, 2, 2, 1, etc. The second part of the test, when I heard the word *one*, I would click. When I heard the word *two*, I would not click. Then in the third part of the test, you would either hear the word or the word would flash on the screen. If you heard the word *one* or if the number 1 flashed on the screen, you had to click. If you heard the word *two* or the number 2 flashed n the screen, you would not click. The therapist was sitting in the corner watching. I think she was there to assess if I was having trouble staying focused, because I definitely found myself looking around the room a bit. I guess I flunked that test – I mean, it showed that I indeed had ADHD. Of course, it's all on a scale. I don't think I'm too bad compared to others. The bigger beast for me is my OCD, but the two are definitely interrelated. I definitely know I have ADHD. It's just the little sister to my OCD.

I can focus on certain things much easier than others. When I'm talking to people, I tend to be very focused. Our standardized patients[32], for instance – we take their medical histories and perform clinical exams – and I really enjoy these experiences in medical school. Conversations are good for me. I can focus better when another person is involved. In social situations, I find that I am able to maintain my focus; but in private situations, like doing schoolwork or taking exams, I tend to really struggle.

---

[32] A Standardized Patient (SP) is a hired, trained actor or actress used to train students of medical, nursing, pharmacy, and physician-assistant schools in simulated patient interactions. These actors are trained by licensed medical institutions to help students master specific skill sets.

I get testing accommodations at school. I take my exams in a small room with only five other students, and I get fifteen extra minutes. The big thing for me is being amongst fewer people. Before I was granted accommodations, I used to walk into the big lecture hall with all one-hundred-and-forty students about to begin a high-stakes exam, and everyone would be stressing out so much. I could feel the tension in the air, and I'm a person who feeds off other people's energy, and so in that big lecture hall with all one-hundred-and-forty students with anxiety levels of eight/nine/ten, it was extremely uncomfortable for me. If someone starts quizzing me right before an exam, or if I hear people quizzing each other and I don't know the answer, it can create a level of anxiety in me that I can't get rid of. And during the exam, whenever a student stands up, I have to watch them. If I hear a weird cough, I have to locate the person coughing. It is a more relaxed environment in a room with only four or five students. It doesn't feel as crazy. I walk into that room and there isn't that terrible level of anxiety. And so environment really affects me. It's very much a mental game for me.

I use a lot of different study techniques. Because of my ADHD, or my OCD, or just because I'm me – I'll start one thing and then get distracted and start something else, and then I won't finish either. As someone who tends to squirrel from topic to topic, it's helpful for me to take different approaches to the same material. I just can't pay attention to any one type of learning for too long. So just realizing that there are various ways to learn the same information, and different sources, and different methods of the material being presented, has been really helpful for me. One trick I have incorporated into my studying is using a timer. I'll study cardiology for forty minutes, take a ten-minute break, then study anatomy for forty minutes, take another ten-minute break. For me, anxiety can snowball. Another thing I've learned is that instead of focusing on my racing thoughts, I try to focus my attention on what I can see. I'm looking at my friend. He's wearing glasses, and he has a beard, and we're sitting at a table, and there are runners on the table, and there's a lamp over there, and the light is on, and it's illuminating a calendar. I'm not stopping my thoughts from racing, but I'm redirecting them to something more neutral.

Above all else, I have learned that I need to make time to care for myself, because my anxiety and my ADHD are significantly worse when I'm sad or sleep deprived. I'm not as productive if I'm in one of those negative moods. And so I might go for a walk, or call somebody, or take a long bath and listen to some Latin music. I know that I have to talk about these things. I'm a very extroverted person. Talking to people is therapeutic for me, and sometimes I just need someone to listen. Sometimes I just want someone to tell me that they understand, and that what I'm going through sounds really difficult. It can be comforting to have somebody you care about validate your feelings.

I just get so overwhelmed with school. At the beginning of the year, when I was adjusting to the shock of medical school, I was probably only getting four or five hours of sleep a night. Now I get seven or eight hours of sleep a night. It's a very important thing for me. Caffeine and anxiety don't really mix to well, so I don't drink coffee or energy drinks, and I'm not a huge black tea fan. I drink diet coke. It's my caffeine of choice. As far as alcohol, I'm quite aware that when I drink my anxiety levels go up. I made a conscious decision when I was younger not to drink until I turned twenty-one. I know – golden child, whatever – but I had no idea know how my mind would respond to being drunk.

That sophomore year of college when my OCD got really bad, I was taking an anatomy course. There were timed lab practicals, just like we have now, but it was horrible because I couldn't stop performing rituals in my head. We would have one minute at each station to identify whatever bodily structure a pin was sticking into, and during the first thirty seconds I'd be performing these rituals. Sometimes I would spend the whole minute performing rituals. Then the alarm would ring, I would rotate to the next station, and I would have to start the ritual all over again.

Eventually, during that sophomore year of college, my symptoms got to the point where I wouldn't even get out of bed. I stopped showering. I thought that whatever obtrusive thought I was having would enter my body through the food I was eating, so I just stopped eating. People started telling me how great I looked. What's your secret? they would ask. It was then that I realized that being skinny is only positive when it comes from a healthy place and from healthy practices. Sure, it was great being skinny, but I was so unhappy. I would rather be big and happy than skinny and depressed. The first therapist I saw in college was an eating disorder specialist and she diagnosed me with an eating disorder. We just didn't mesh. She didn't know how to deal with OCD, and I didn't have an eating disorder. I only lost weight because of my OCD.

I've lost some weight in medical school too, but mostly because I forget to eat. We're just so busy. Days are long, and I only bring so much food to school with me. I've always struggled a bit with my weight. I have hypothyroidism[33], which is not a mental health problem, but it does have to do with hormones in the body. I found out about my hypothyroidism when I was kid and I had a difficult time sleeping. I remember having a lot of anxiety over the fact that everybody else was sleeping and I wasn't. I just couldn't fall asleep. And I was having bad abdominal pain. My parents took me to a pediatric gastrointestinal specialist, and one day my mom happened to mention to him that we have a history of thyroid disease. They checked my thyroid levels and I was off the charts. So then I was diagnosed, and treated, and I started sleeping better after that, and I became a more normal sized ten-year-old.

---

[33] Thyroid hormones are required for the normal development of the nervous system. In hypothyroid infants, synapses develop abnormally, myelination is defective, and mental retardation occurs. Hypothyroid adults have several reversible neurologic abnormalities, including slowed mentation, forgetfulness, decreased hearing, and ataxia. Some patients have severe mental symptoms, including reversible dementia or overt psychosis ("myxedema madness"). The cerebrospinal fluid protein level is abnormally high; however, total cerebral blood flow and oxygen consumption are normal. Deep tendon reflexes are sluggish, with a slowed ("hung-up") relaxation phase. Paresthesias are common, often caused by compression neuropathies resulting from an accumulation of myxedema (carpal tunnel syndrome and tarsal tunnel syndrome). Hypothyroidism is associated with muscle weakness, cramps, and stiffness.

I feel like my body is this big science experiment. All these things are going on in me, and being an osteopathic medical student, I get to analyze myself as I learn the pathophysiology of my disorders. You know why I decided to become an osteopathic physician? It's because I think D.O.'s approach medicine with – and I mean it when I say this – a more holistic approach. I think M.D.'s appreciate this too, but a patient is more than just the physical issues they come in with. I can use myself as an example. I have hypothyroidism. This is technically a physical issue. But some things that I experience due to my hypothyroidism, for instance weight gain, influence my emotional health. The entire body is interconnected. There's more to it than just treating the physical issues. Learning about our patients is invaluable. Unfortunately, the way the medical system works today, we just don't have time to get to know our patients or where they're coming from. There are so many things that patients might not think about mentioning to us that might be affecting their health. I really like how osteopathy tries to incorporate all of these different facets into treatment. Learning how a person lives, what's going on in their family, with their kids, with their pets – all of these things influence how a person is feeling, and that influences their health.

The way I see, we're given one life. Everyone has different values – but for me, it's about the people and the relationships I get to make. This is why I think I want to go into family medicine. It's a specialization that allows you to know your patients and to be really involved in their lives. I want to help them. I'm very interested in health, but there's so much that is involved in a person, and the thoughts they think, and the things they do, and the people they love. It's a privilege to be an osteopathic medical student. It's a really unique thing that we get to do. Dealing with mental health disorders like OCD and ADHD has made me that much more compassionate, that much more adept at relating to people on a very specific level.

Yes, sometimes you will feel hopeless. I remember the feeling of hopelessness – that my OCD would never get better, and there was nothing I could do about it. But if I can accept my own limitations, and accept that this is the way I am, then I might be able to help others. Because a lot of my obsessive thoughts revolve around empathy and compassion for others. This is the gift of my OCD. I'm a more empathetic person because of it. Before I struggled with it, I don't know if I could necessarily relate to someone with a mental health issue. If you haven't dealt with something like this, it can be hard to understand why it's a struggle.

> *Just snap out of it.*
> *Make yourself get out of bed!*
> *Why don't you go and take a shower?*
> *Why is this such an issue?*
> *I don't get it.*

But I've lived it. I've been there. I totally understand why that's a problem. And so you just can't ever give up.

I suffer from mental health problems, and as a future physician I think a big part of my career is going to be trying to make behavioral health less stigmatized. Lots of people I know could probably benefit from mental health counseling. These are people who I'm really close with. And I'm sure they feel like – oh, it's fine. I'm not *that* bad. I don't need *that*. Sometimes it makes me sad when I realize that I need to go back to therapy. It feels like I'm regressing. But it's not a matter of regressing – it's about educating yourself to what's happening with *you*. It's about accepting that this is just another disease. I've felt depressed realizing that I'm never going to be cured. I will never wake up one day and not have OCD. If I break my arm, well, in six months, I'm going to be okay again. But OCD is something that I'm going to live with until the day I die. It can feel discouraging. But I've accepted that this is a part of me. And I'm in a good position to try and help people realize that behavioral health is something you can work on. It's only a piece of you, and it can actually contribute to making you into a really great and special person.

# NEELOU

*I've learned to accept that it's okay to be anxious rather than trying never to be anxious. This is who I am. I'm an anxious person. It's not going to kill me.*

***Generalized Anxiety Disorder***
***Panic Disorder***

I BEGAN EXPERIENCING really bad anxiety and depression very early in my first semester of medical school. I wasn't sleeping. I stopped eating. I stopped showering. I had never experienced panic attacks before, but it got to where I was having them every ten minutes when I was at school. The moment I would see the school, it would hit me. I wasn't able to go to class like that. I started falling further and further behind. I was suffering more and more anxiety. After dealing with it for over a month, and going to the hospital, and consulting with Student Affairs, we all decided that I should just go home. So, yes, it was in my first semester of medical school that I experienced my first panic attack. And then I left.

\* \* \*

I was an emo kid[34] in middle school. In high school I was really rebellious. I ditched class all the time. I wore low-cut shirts, had blonde highlights in my hair. I went by the name of Nellie; it was my alter-ego. It's funny, but these days when I tell people that I was like that, they don't believe me. I guess I'm pretty different now.

I went to Santa Cruz for college and studied molecular biology. I was that Type A[35] student who had to get good grades. I *had* to have a really good GPA, so I was always anxious about exams. I've been an anxious person all my life. When I graduated from college, I decided I didn't want to live my life like that anymore. I didn't want to follow the pre-med handbook. I was at a fork in the road. I had been offered a job at Harvard University; alternatively, I realized that I could just pack up my things and move somewhere

---

[34] The origin of the word 'emo' comes from 1980s alternative hardcore rock music and is closely associated with punk bands and indie scene music. Many people see emo as an off-shoot of the hardcore goth or punk scene, with its own subculture and style.

[35] Type A personality is characterized as competitive, time urgent, hostile, and aggressive. Type A individuals tend to be self-critical and strive toward goals without feeling a sense of joy in their efforts or accomplishments. Often times, these individuals have poor life balance, and are easily 'wound up.'

totally new, somewhere where I didn't know a single person, where I could just start living my life.

I grew up in a rather conservative Persian family – well, maybe not conservative – but I grew up *Persian*. And good Persian girls don't just move off by themselves. But I did it. I packed up my things and moved to Alaska! And it was the best decision of my life. I was thriving, and mentally I was doing great. People say that college is the happiest time of your life, but for me it was one of my lowest. I didn't have a typical college experience. I was always studying. But in Alaska, I was just so happy. It was the happiest time of my life.

When I moved there I didn't have a job, so I started working at a clothing store in the mall in Anchorage. Then I got a job with the American Lung Association. In most of Alaska, there isn't a comprehensive smoke-free policy in housing, nor in the bars or restaurants. So I started worked in tobacco prevention with the University of Alaska. I became an advocate of smoke-free housing projects. It was really rewarding.

I always knew I wanted to go to medical school. Anxiety never even crossed my mind. I *never* thought I would struggle. If anything, I assumed I would be top of my class. My top choice medical schools were in the Pacific Northwest because I knew I wanted to return to Alaska. There are no medical schools in Alaska, but there are two schools that have rotation sites in Alaska. So I applied, and I was accepted. Of course, I dreaded leaving. I was so happy in Alaska. I felt a lot of stress coming from my boyfriend too. He was Alaskan and didn't want to do the long-distance relationship thing. I was basically trying to force it on him. So, no, I wasn't happy about moving. I didn't want to go to Washington State. But it was time to go. So once again I packed up my things and moved back down to the Lower Forty-Eight. I had to. Medical school was starting. It was stressful for me from the very start.

And then it escalated.

In the beginning I was fine. I was trying hard to adjust to my new life as a first-year medical student while trying to make my boyfriend happy. I could tell he wasn't happy though. Things were going okay for me. I was getting good grades. But by the middle of September, I noticed I was having tremors in my hands. I thought I was drinking too much coffee. Then I started having trouble sleeping. I was shaking all the time. I wasn't myself at all, and it was getting worse. Then we had the first *Hell Week*. There are periods in medical school where high-stake exams are stacked in daily succession. I think we had seven exams back-to-back. It was at the end of September. It went downhill from there. I was studying all day and all night. I was crying all the time. It must have really been stressful on my parents. I just wasn't the Neelou I had been before. I was always sad. Whenever someone asked me how school was going, I would jokingly say, 'I hate my life.' I was completely depressed. I stopped showering, and I think that was the biggest trigger, me not showering. In a sense, I was going to school all dirty. I realized that I wasn't even able to take care of myself. I just didn't have enough time. It continued to build and build until it got really bad. I started having the panic attacks.

It is a very frightening experience to have a panic attack. Your heart starts pounding. You're dizzy. You're shaking. Sweating. Tingling. I've thrown up before. I've fainted. I remember driving myself to the hospital once while my whole body was tingling. My heart pounding. I thought I was having a heart attack. I remember not being able to breathe. It was one of the most frightening things I had ever experienced. The panic attacks were caused primarily because of the academic pressure. Of course, it didn't help that my boyfriend wasn't – I don't want to say unsupportive, but he just didn't understand. He never wanted to talk. The panic attacks evolved into a perpetual state of panic. The only thing I could do to calm down was walk the hallways. I spent hours walking up and down those hallways.

I stopped going to school. The Student Affairs office excused me and I just stopped going. You know, you can make it through medical school without going to most classes. Lots of students do it. But then I began missing exams. My grades started to fall. I remember it was a Saturday morning when I called the Student Affairs coordinator and told her that I needed to leave. For good. My mom has really bad anxiety too – *really* bad anxiety – and I knew if I told her it could be bad. She was in Paris at the time. So I called my dad and he just said, 'Okay. Come home.'

The Associate Dean signed my paperwork that Monday and I left. I moved back to San Jose with my dad. It was early October and my world was turned upside down. Medical school is all-encompassing, and my life had been medical school. All of a sudden, I was back home. *What do I do now? Do I get a job? I was so happy just a few months ago.*

But the panic attacks stopped. Then the depression began.

I was crying all the time. I entered a stage where I wouldn't get out of bed. I only left the house to go to therapy. I started seeing a psychiatrist and a mindfulness therapist. Then two weeks after I returned home, my dad had a cardiac arrest[36]. It was absolutely horrifying. He was playing tennis and his heart just stopped. It was stopped for two minutes. He would have died, but his young tennis coach had thought to bring a defibrillator that day. He saved my dad's life. My mom was in Paris, my brother was at college, and I was in San Jose with my dad. So I suppose that in a way my panic attacks were a kind of blessing. Because they brought me home when my dad needed me. He was in a coma, but he came back. Now his heart is beating even better than before.

My therapist and I were mostly dealing with my leaving medical school, but after my father's cardiac arrest we started focusing on that. I still have

---

[36] Cardiac arrest is defined as an abrupt loss of heart function that may come suddenly or in the wake of other symptoms. Cardiac arrest is different than heart attack. Heart attack is caused by a blockage that stops blood flow to the heart. Cardiac arrest is caused when the heart's electrical system malfunctions.

nightmares about it. And I still work with my therapist. It's an ongoing process. I meditate a lot these days. I use breathing techniques. I practice yoga. My dad's rehab facility had all these different anxiety de-stressor programs. So when he was in rehab, I was in a mindfulness workshop in the same hospital. We even did a laughing yoga class together.

Eventually, my psychiatrist put me on *Lexapro*[37]. I've been on it for almost two years now. I guess I got really lucky because it worked. She got it right on the first try. Well, I should say that for the first two weeks it did give me insomnia. But now it's just a pill that I take every morning.

I started changing things in my life, so that I would be better able to handle medical school. It was a combination of changes. I used to drink maybe ten cups of coffee a day. I've taught myself to stop drinking coffee at one o'clock now. If I'm feeling especially stressed, I try to take a quick nap. It restarts me. I've

---

[37] *Lexapro (trade name),* Escitalopram *(generic).* The SSRIs (selective serotonin reuptake inhibitors) are a class of drugs that include fluoxetine, sertraline, paroxetine, fluvoxamine, citalopram and its enantiomer: escitalopram. The chief advantages of these agents are that they are generally well tolerated, the starting dose is typically a therapeutic dose for most patients, and they have much lower lethality in overdose compared to TCAs (tricyclic antidepressants) or MAO (Monoamine oxidase) inhibitors.

incorporated running into my life. Last year I would walk the hallways of the school back and forth for hours. Running has a similar effect, only better. You would think that exercise would speed your heart up – and of course it does – but then it tires me out and my heart rate falls and maybe it's harder to feel anxious when your body is physically tired. Exercise, proper sleep, and moderate intake of stimulants – these have been important elements that I have integrated into my life.

Sure, *Lexapro* works really well for me, and Cognitive Behavioral Therapy has taught me techniques that I can actively use, and of course mindfulness – whenever I feel stressed now, I tell myself that it's going to be over soon. It is not permanent. Just three more days. Things will get better. And I've learned that panic attacks won't kill me. I didn't know this before. You won't die from a panic attack. If my heart starts to race, I recognize that it's only a reflex. Nothing terrible is going to happen. This mindset has been really positive. Last week, for instance, I was having pretty bad anxiety, and I kept telling myself: *This is only temporary. You're going to be okay. This is your heart just doing its thing. Sometimes your heart races.* This shift in mentality has really worked for me. I've learned to accept that it's okay to be anxious rather than trying never to be anxious. This is who I am. I'm an anxious person. It's not going to kill me.

I was super nervous about going back to medical school. My family was worried too. But in August of 2018, I started first-year medical school for the second time. I was *really* self-conscious about being back. I was so embarrassed. I didn't know what people were going to think. I would avoid going to school unless I had to be there for lecture. I tried to avoid walking through the foyer because I didn't want to see any of the second-years. I'm sure they all knew why I had left, but I didn't want to see anyone. I would put my head down, pull my hood up, and walk as quickly as I could.

The first students who I told – that I was originally from the previous class – were in my SciFoM group. We were a group of three students and we had to work together during interactive classroom sessions. I told two others whom I had become close with. And then other students started to find out. At this point, I wanted to help students who were nervous. So when someone was wondering what exams were going to be like, for instance, I didn't want to pretend I didn't know. I started telling people about my experience, and about what to expect, and how to study. So, yes, my classmates slowly started to find out, but what I noticed was that they didn't care. I thought they would judge me or ask why I had left – but no one cared. I remember saying to my psychiatrist, 'They literally do not care that I was from the previous class.' She said, 'Why would you think they would?'

I've learned in therapy that emotions are fluid. I'm never going to be happy all the time. Life is a process. It isn't a stagnant thing. I'm going to have good days and I'm going to have bad days. Last week was a bad week. This week is a better week. I didn't have this mentality last year during my first go-round of medical school. And so, honestly, with all the mindfulness techniques I've incorporated into my life, and after meeting all my new classmates, the transition just sort of flowed.

I've also realized that many of my classmates, and many people in general, suffer from anxiety. It's helpful being open about it, especially if you're going through such an anxiety-inducing experience as medical school. Even though most of us are Type A students, we each have flaws. We all have imperfections. I want people to feel comfortable talking to each other about these things, because the worst thing I did last year was to not talk about what I was experiencing and how I was feeling. It was the worst thing I could have done.

The advice I would give to someone who maybe just had their first panic attack, and they're scared, is to recognize that panic attacks can't hurt you. Understand that your emotions are fluid. It's normal to feel like this. It's normal to have anxiety. You have to ride it out. Don't try to fight it. Just ride it out. Go for a walk. Talk to someone about it. Know that it can't hurt you.

A couple months ago – we were toward the end of our cardiology block in the middle of second semester – I started feeling the symptoms coming on. My heart was starting to beat faster. I started sweating. I felt the tingling. All those same feelings were coming back, but I didn't ignore it like I used to. I embraced it. I knew it wasn't going to hurt me, and by embracing it, it didn't trigger the same response that it had before. I used to let the panic consume me. But now I understand what was happening with my body, physically and emotionally, and I just let it happen. It's only temporary. There's only so fast your heart can beat before your sympathetic reflex kicks off and your heart rate starts to fall. It's not going to kill you. This is going to pass. You're going to be okay. You got this.

# AUGUSTUS

*The whole trick is to continue to remind yourself that ADHD, and many other mental health problems, they're not necessarily disorders – they're just different perspectives. If handled correctly, you can use them to their advantage.*

## *Attention Deficit Hyperactivity Disorder*

A LOT OF PEOPLE joke about how ADD[38] they are, suggesting that they are perfectionists in some regard. The condition is actually rather prevalent in our society. I'm a first-year medical student, twenty-five years old, and I live with ADHD. I was probably seven years old when I was diagnosed.

I showed a lot of the classic symptoms as a child: I was disruptive in class, I wouldn't pay attention, I wouldn't get my work done – and yet my teachers always said that I was a smart kid. I could get things done when I was given things that actually kept me engaged. For instance, I would be given extra sheets of multiplication tables to work on so that I wouldn't disrupt the class too much. When I was in first or

---

[38] Kids with this condition [ADD] aren't hyperactive. They don't have the high energy level seen in others with ADHD. These children can be described as shy or "in their own world."

second grade, my mother was prompted by the school principal to seek out a doctor concerning possible ADHD. We went to a physician and I was formally diagnosed. It was a bit of a shock to my mom. She didn't know how to take it. I was the only person in my family diagnosed.

People are quick to jump to the conclusion that a disruptive kid must have ADHD. There tends not to be enough scrutinizing what might actually be manifesting in that kid. Of course, in my case, it *did* pan out to be ADHD – but a lot of kids who are diagnosed probably don't have ADHD. They get started on medication and the underlying problem isn't being addressed.

At age seven, I just didn't know what it meant to have ADHD. When I was about eight, my parents decided to start experimenting with *Ritalin*[39], so I started taking one 5 mg *Ritalin* a day. When that wasn't working, I started taking two pills a day. Eventually, I was taking three pills a day, for a total of 15 mg. When that still wasn't working, and I think I was eleven, I was switched to a higher potency stimulant called *Concerta*[40].

---

[39] Ritalin (trade name), Methylphenidate (generic). Methylphenidate, amphetamine, and methamphetamine are psychostimulants approved in the United States for treatment of attention-deficit hyperactivity disorder (ADHD), weight control, and narcolepsy.

*Concerta* is a 54 mg pill, a big jump from 15 mg of *Ritalin*. It was a lot for a kid.

But then I noticed positive changes right away. My parents noticed it too. I became more focused and stopped disrupting the class. I was just able to keep my comments to myself. I could stay on task and get my work done. Being on medication compared to being off medication, you could distinguish a noticeable dichotomy to my character. On meds, I was a focused, respectable, and good student. People would tell my parents what a good kid I was. Off meds, I was little nightmare.

'Did you take your pills today?'

It's a phrase that kids with ADHD hear a lot. My parents would sense when I was acting 'off,' and they would ask me, 'Did you take your pills today?' Being so young and on medication, it can be difficult to keep to a consistent regiment. Initially, I used a pill

---

[40] Concerta (trade name), Methylphenidate (generic). Stimulant medications, specifically Methylphenidate and amphetamine-based formulations, are the mainstays of AD/HD therapy. Their mode of action appears to be blocking of dopamine transporters. Historically, the most commonly prescribed treatment has been immediate-release Methylphenidate given two to three times per day in doses of 5–20 mg. Methylphenidate typically begins working in 30–60 minutes, with effects peaking at 1–2 hours and an overall duration of 2–5 hours.

dispenser that would designate my pill for the day. Over time I became more responsible and self-reliant. These days, when I get up in the morning, my pills are right next to me on the nightstand; I grab them, pop one, and I'm on my way.

It can be a scary thing for a kid, being told that you have this disorder and you need to take medicine for it. My grandma says that when I was young, about the time I was diagnosed, I said to her one day – 'I don't need to take my pills anymore, Grandma, because I'm normal, just like you.' She says she got a little emotional right then. Other than that, I think I've always realized that medication is something positive that can help me be more successful. Becoming accustomed to ADHD and medication at so young an age, and understanding that it's just another part of me, has been very beneficial.

I have friends and acquaintances with ADHD who started on medication much later in life, and like most of us, they experienced their own trials and tribulations regarding whether they should take pills or not take pills. For me, the reason why I stay on them is because I can feel the difference; when I'm off them – I don't want to say *withdrawal*, but I feel very different. I've been on them so long now that when I run out, which I try hard not to do, I feel very lethargic. All I want to do is sleep. I'll be trying to stay on task, and it's not a matter of me concentrating, but more so just trying to stay awake. It's one of the factors that keeps me on meds. If I don't take my pill, I experience this crazy kind of *withdrawal*; it's a bad word, so let's say *side effect* instead.

Now, there have been more conventional side effects, like high blood pressure, which doctors attribute to the medication. And I think the meds can sometimes make me overly preoccupied with trivial things. They're supposed to help me stay focused, but people with ADHD can become kind of super-focused, and you might not be able to switch it off. You can get stuck on something that you're not trying to focus on. But other than these little side-effects, the medication is great. I don't notice too much of a negative, which is probably why I've been on it for so long.

It is a constant battle. You never really overcome the hump of 'I have a disorder.' Today, for instance, we had a big exam – an anatomy lab practical. There were times during the practical where I thought, *Man, I wish I would have studied more; I wish I would have focused on this other topic more.* You go through this cycle of self-doubt – reassurance – self-doubt –

reassurance. The trick to ADHD is realizing that you have to get up one more time than you get knocked down. You experience these feelings of inadequacy, and so realize that it's not *you* that is inadequate, it's just that you have a different perspective on life than most people. When you look around, people are probably not going to understand, or you're going to *think* that they don't understand – who you are, or what you're doing – and you're going to *think* that they're normal and you're not normal. You're going to think they're more successful. They're doing everything right. You're doing everything wrong. This is the wrong perspective to have, but you're going to have it anyway. The whole trick is to continue to remind yourself that ADHD, and many other mental health problems, they're not necessarily disorders – they're just different perspectives. If handled correctly, you can use them to their advantage.

I used to hole myself up in a little cubicle in the science building of my college, and I wouldn't move for six or seven hours. I would just straight study. I would barely eat, barely drink, and I would be so preoccupied with what I was doing that I would completely lose track of time. I was very productive of course. People would walk by and catch me off guard. 'Augustus, *what are you doing?* You're studying too hard. Take a break, man.' They'd ask me how I could sit there for so long. But for me, it was nothing. I wasn't doing anything different from anyone else. I was just sitting there studying. But to them, I was in some crazy focused mode.

When something peeks your interest, or maybe it's something you're passionate about, you can enter into a hyper-focused state. It can be a huge advantage if you can point the direction of this hyper-focus. But it's like a cannon – you can't expect to have great accuracy with a cannon. All you can do is kind of point it. I've found it very useful for me to point my hyper-focus, and now that I'm in medicine it's even more useful, because there are a lot of things about medicine that really fascinate me. Medical school isn't like undergrad where there are countless topics you have to study that just don't strike your interest. In medical school, every day I find something where I think, *Oh my gosh, this is amazing!* So you have to find your niche, and then aim your focus. This is where people with ADHD can be really successful.

---

[41] Cognitive Behavioral Therapy (CBT) is a form of psychological treatment that has been demonstrated to be as effective as, or more effective, than other psychological therapy or psychiatric medications. CBT is based on cover principles: psychological problems are based on faulty or unhelpful ways of thinking or behavior. These problems can improve using more effective coping mechanisms to change thinking patterns.

One of the biggest things people with ADHD can do is to learn how to manage it with cognitive behavioral therapy[41]. CBT teaches you to create an internal filter. It's like having a coach throughout your day reminding you that even though you might have something really interesting you want to blurt out, maybe it's not an appropriate time to speak. You learn how to censure and advise yourself. *Hey, just hold off. Be quiet. Don't say anything yet.* Maybe you're in class and you're losing focus, and so you learn how to come up with little games to reengage yourself. *If I color-code this, then maybe I can concentrate on this topic better.* You might promise yourself that if you get through the next ten minutes, then you can go for a jog. These are behavioral devices you can learn through CBT. Having that little coach in your head and learning these little tricks can be more helpful than medication alone.

My mom taught high school psychology. Maybe she implanted some of these techniques into my head or maybe there were aspects of her influence that I simply picked up on, but when I actually learned about CBT in high school, I realized there were techniques that I was already kind of doing. I started looking into it more. What tips are there out there for people like me? What tricks can I learn? I did a lot of research. I still do a lot of research. I look for suggestions from people living with ADHD. I try to identify things that have helped make them successful, because there are many people out there who more than get by with ADHD.

The founder of JetBlue[42] has ADHD. He describes it as a big part of what has made him successful. The spontaneous outbursts that I have learned to control are things that I pick up on, thoughts that suddenly hit me, and some of them are really good ideas. I was very artistic growing up. I still am. I know that my having ADHD has made me who I am. I'm a person who thinks outside the box when lots of people are maybe following a straight line. In this sense, I'm thankful that I have ADHD. It has given me these special gifts.

I have always been athletic. I was a collegiate athlete, but I've never thought of my ADHD as helping in my athletic life. I suppose you do see a correlation though. Michael Phelps[43], for instance, has ADHD. But

---

[42] JetBlue Airways Corporation was created by Utah entrepreneur David Neeleman, to 'bring the humanity back to air travel.' It was also a good way to add another chapter to a successful career in budget air travel. Jet Blue was launched with a huge amount capital, brand new planes, and expert personnel in key positions. It grew rapidly as customers flocked to it to escape the steep fares and frequent delays of the major airlines.

[43] Michael Phelps holds the record for winning the most Olympic

it's probably not because a person has ADHD that he or she is a great athlete; it's probably just happenchance. Sure, it does give me a lot of energy, and of course there is the hyper-focus aspect of it: if I'm really interested in something, I'm going to work really hard at it. I grew up really loving to play baseball and football. I remember going outside and hitting buckets and buckets of baseballs, working on my swing, working on my technique. I remember working out and working out, trying to build up particular muscles, because I was so focused on getting better. I would outtrain all my teammates because —well, probably my ADHD was kicking in, so I suppose it was actually an advantage.

The medication I take is a stimulant related to methamphetamine. *Methylphenidate*[44] is the chemical name. You hear how these sorts of stimulants are the steroids of medical school, or of any academia – but I don't think this is the proper way to consider medication. I believe that the best way to deal with a mental health disorder is to assess it for yourself before jumping straight to any kind of med. I take

---

events in history, with 28 medals, including 23 gold. "Phelps was diagnosed with ADHD in sixth grade. But while he couldn't sit through class without fidgeting, he could swim for up to three hours at the pool after school."

[44] Concerta is trade name for Methylphenidate.

*methylphenidate* because I need it to function properly. I've grown accustomed to it over the years. Now in the world of ADHD medication and users, I feel like kind of a goody-two-shoes because I've never tried to abuse my meds. Abusing any medication, even to reach a state of hyper-focus for academic purposes, is probably not the best way of handling a drug.

When I entered medical school, I had to learn how to be more organized than I had ever been before. I had to learn to be even more focused. I had to change what I was doing in the past to become more successful in the present. In effecting this change, I wasn't motivated to alter my medication or even to up the dosage. The medication is great in helping establish my baseline. I used to see a therapist who had the perfect description of my medication. She told me that I'm like a wave-form, with crazy highs where I'm super focused and crazy lows where I'm not focused at all, and the purpose of the medication is to bring me to a more neutral straight line. I might not get the benefits of a hyper-focused state of mind, but I also don't experience the negative side-effects. It brings me to baseline. And once you reach your baseline, you're not going to benefit by uping the dosage.

What you can do is cognitive behavioral therapy. You can simplify. You can look at aspects of your life and work to get rid of some of the snags of ADHD. For instance, I would often lose things. I think a lot of people with ADHD lose things. They get sidetracked. Where did I put my keys? Where did I put my badge? I've taught myself to leave my badge with my keys in the exact same place whenever I come home. Another thing, and I get a lot of ridicule for this, but I love it – I have a ginormous backpack. I have everything I need for the day in my backpack: my workout clothes at the bottom, all my books, my laptop, all my chargers stored away in nice little pouches, everything organized.

Organization is key!

Being diagnosed is the first step. There are people out there who are remiss to admit that they have ADHD. They are diagnosed but they don't cope with it. Some people are ashamed of it. They might feel that they have to hide who they are. This is not the right way to go about dealing with a diagnosis, because now you're ignoring the problem. Developing the techniques to better manage the diagnosis is the second step. And once the techniques become second nature, you realize that you can be more successful than you ever imagined. I attribute so much of my success to the organizational skills I have learned.

Because I learned to understand my ADHD from a very early age, I came to view the world from a very particular lens. I would observe people. I would watch what they were doing and how they were reacting. I would pick up on little idiosyncrasies about them. Having ADHD made me feel like kind of an outsider, but I acquired the skill of reading people and trying to understand how they think. I'm not saying that I'm the best person to navigate difficult situations, but I do know that it has made me very effective in certain roles. I often pick up on when something is wrong. I frequently see when people are 'off.' I want to help them find their best self and get back to baseline. Maybe this is why I went into medicine.

With ADHD, you're constantly cycling through highs and lows. Prior to medical school, I went through a period where I believed I wasn't good enough. I had the grades for it, I had a great MCAT score, I was accepted into the school I wanted to get into – but I just didn't think I was good enough. I remember searching online and I came across a medical student's blog. The student chronicled his journey with ADHD from the time of his diagnosis, which was during his undergraduate years, his coming to terms with it, and then learning how to deal with the medications. He described how he overcame the difficulties and was able to succeed as a medical student. It was very inspiring and motivational. It instilled in me a confidence that, one, someone with ADHD can do medical school. It is completely possible. Two, here's a guy who was just recently diagnosed, was going through all the troubles of learning how to deal with his ADHD, and all the while he was balancing medical school. If he was able to do it, and I'm coming into medical school already understanding my ADHD to some extent, I can definitely do it. And, three, it simply gave me hope.

Recognizing that you have ADHD opens you up to a part of yourself that you can now begin to understand. This is perhaps the biggest thing you can do. The first step, and the biggest step, is realizing that you have something that makes you unique. It makes you diverse – I like to say *neuro*-diverse – and this is not a bad thing. It can actually be a very good thing. You can use it effectively by learning techniques, and you can learn to adjust the way you study. You can learn how to adjust your daily life. These changes can make you into a more successful person. And so for anybody recently diagnosed with ADHD, I would want them to know that it's not the end of the world – in fact, it's a new world.

# DANIELLA

*I felt really duped. Even if I knew it wouldn't be picture-perfect, I had no idea how isolating it would be. I didn't know it could hit you so hard. Parenthood is supposed to be so wonderful.*

***Major Depressive Disorder***
***Postpartum Depression***

WHEN I SAY 'DEPRESSION,' I picture one of those commercials where somebody is standing by a rainy window and everything looks all gloomy around them. Yes, it can be like that, but let's take it back to the real world – and let me warn you: I am brutally honest. It's taboo to acknowledge some of the things that I experienced, but I'm going to tell you anyway.

\* \* \*

I'm a non-traditional first-year medical student – non-traditional because I came to medical school from the business world, and because I'm a mother of a two-and-a-half-year-old. I lived a bit of a crazy life before this. Then one day I was like, *I don't want to do this anymore. I want to go to medical school.* I don't know why I made that conscious decision. I was working at a big company and the VP of marketing walked by and said something about having to pick up a Maserati as a loaner, something like that, and I remember thinking, *I don't want to be like that.* Medical school popped into my head for some reason. I decided right then and there; it was very spur of the moment. I thought it over for a few weeks. Are you serious about this? Do you even remember how to read a textbook? I was twenty-five years old when I made that decision.

From an outsider perspective, I was living the dream. I was successful in the business world; I was going back to school; I was married to a handsome man from Texas; I had given birth to a healthy baby boy – and eventually I gained a seat into a medical school. I had everything I had ever asked for. Sometimes I have to remind myself, especially when people allude to the fact that I have all these great things going for me, that I worked my ass off. It was a constant battle. Every which way and all along, from deciding to leave the business world to being right here today, it has been a struggle.

My depression started in college. What happened was that my college sweetheart, a man I dated for four plus years – he was in the Marine Corps and was deployed. I'm sure a lot of things contributed to the depression, but the trauma of the man I loved at the time suddenly being deployed, I think it was a trigger. I didn't come from a military family. I didn't know that kind of experience. It was really hard for me. This was in 2005 during the Iraq War, and it was on the news all the time. This many marines have died today. This many infantrymen have died today. And they didn't have communication bases set up very well. I could send emails, and I think the Red Cross would print them and deliver them, but it wasn't as easy for him to write back to me.

Then I moved to Russia. I was a double foreign-language major in college, so I went to Russia and Spain to study abroad. I was twenty years old and my Russian was terrible. I would find an internet café, send my sweetheart an email, and then just wait. All I could do was hope that I might hear back from him. Although I handled the isolation fine, I was already showing signs of depression. I think I've always been … I don't want to say a loner, but I've always enjoyed my own company. But while I was in Russia, for some reason I wasn't able to handle things too well. People would make me terribly angry. I used to get so angry that I would shake. I wasn't sure what was going on with me. Finally, I came home to the States. And my sweetheart returned too, safe from his deployment.

I remember we were sitting in my room one day at school. Out of nowhere I heard a little voice. It was as if somebody was whispering into my ear. *I think you should cut yourself. You'll feel better.* I turned to my boyfriend. 'Something is going on with me,' I said to him. 'I just heard a weird voice, and I swear I'm not crazy, but that just happened.'

I was really lucky because he took it seriously. He didn't judge me. He called my dad, and my dad said that we needed to get me to a professional immediately. So my boyfriend drove me to my hometown in Yakima, Washington, and I met with a psychiatrist. He was this old school psychiatrist who smoked a pipe. There were elbow patches on his jacket, an old leather couch in his office. He stroked his beard when he was thinking. I think I made him uncomfortable. He would start smoking his pipe more frantically when I talked.

Because I have a family history of depression, my psychiatrist asked what medications other members of my family were taking. I guess he assumed that what worked for them might work for me. I was prescribed *Zoloft*[45], but I didn't want to go on medication at first. I remember fighting it. Somebody finally said to me, 'If you had diabetes you would take meds. When you have a cold you take meds.' And so I thought, *Oh, it's like my brain has the sniffles.* That's how I thought of it after that. My brain has the sniffles and I'm going to give it some sniffle-medication.

Mental health drugs take longer to start working than you would expect. It's not like taking *Sudafed*[46] where you feel it kick in pretty quick. It was very gradual that I started to feel better. I had been taking Zoloft for two months before I realized that I wasn't shaking anymore. Depression is odd, because it manifests in such different ways in people. When

---

[45] Zoloft (trade name), sertraline (generic). Sertraline was the second SSRI introduced, and is more specific in its effects on the inhibition of serotonin (5-hydroxytryptamine [5HT]) reuptake than fluoxetine. Its effects on the reuptake of norepinephrine and dopamine are modest. Sertraline is more effective than placebo, and is comparable to amitriptyline, fluoxetine, fluvoxamine, imipramine, nortriptyline, and venlafaxine in treating late-life depression. It is tolerated more favorably than imipramine and venlafaxine and demonstrates greater cognitive improvement than nortriptyline or fluoxetine.

[46] Sudafed's main ingredient is pseudoephedrine. It is used as a nasal decongestant. It works by relieving congestion by making nasal passages narrower.

you're on the inside – when it's happening to you – you just don't realize that something is off. You have to wait for somebody to say something, and then hopefully you're willing to acknowledge it.

Depression medication isn't always going to be consistent either. You can develop a tolerance. Meds can start to lose their effectiveness. It really takes having your family around, or your crew, because they're the ones who will notice it. They'll notice it long before you will. To you, everything seems fine. You're being a good little girl, in my case, and taking the medication. But it's one of the hardest things to accept – that when your loved ones finally say something, they're not just being jackasses, and it's not because they don't understand. What they're essentially saying is: Can I help you with this? And hopefully you'll question why they're concerned. What is it about me that is making this person worry?

I went off my meds a couple years later, and for a few years I was doing just great. I was a happy little clam. Then I hit another life stressor. I left the business world and moved to Austin, Texas, where I didn't know anybody. And I don't know if I can attribute it to situational depression or not. I was taking all the pre-medical coursework, which is a heavy academic load, and I also began dating my best friend, which was probably a bad idea. We had a bad breakup. I didn't handle it well.

I spoke to a therapist for a while when I was in college. Therapy works really well for some people, but for me it wasn't super effective. Most of the time, I was just talking out of my ass. I'm an action person. I can sit here and talk about my problems and try cognitive-behavioral therapy, but at the end of the day I want to know what I need to do to make myself better, and that's not how most therapists work. I don't want to sit in a room boohooing about things if I'm not going to actively do something about it.

When I was living in Las Vegas, a psychic I was seeing referred me to a hypnotherapist. The way hypnotherapy works is that they put you in a chair with a blanket, so you feel all warm and comfortable, and then they put you 'under'. Although you're aware of everything that is happening, it's like your subconscious can't resist being more open and receptive. They ask you a question and you *have* to think about it. You can't put up your usual defenses. I remember the back of my brain felt all fuzzy and tingly. It was very surreal. Maybe it sounds creepy, but what the hypnotherapist does is guide a very natural conversation. And then I just started talking. I could hear myself talking. It was like verbal vomiting. All of a sudden, I was saying things that I had no idea I was feeling; memories were surfacing that I had been suppressing for a very long time. When you're in a receptive state of hypnotherapy, you can't pretend that everything is okay when it's not. Something was wrong.

But I was moving forward with my life. Then shortly after that bad breakup, I met the man I would eventually marry. After only dating for about five weeks, I remember I wanted us to get a dog, and – I guess this prompted it – he insisted that we have *The Talk*. But I just wanted a dog. I love dogs. But being a Texas man, he insisted we have *The Talk*. So we did. We talked about where we saw our relationship going, and our life goals, what was debatable and not debatable. My thing was: I wanted to go to medical school. It was non-negotiable. His thing was: he wanted children.

My mom tells me that when I was a little girl, I said to her that I didn't want to be a mom. Kids are exhausting, and I think I understood that even then. They use your money. They cause you headaches. Why put yourself through that? Everybody acts like it's fine, but really ... why have children? The problem was that I really liked Diego. I *really* liked him. So I said, fine, we can have kids. We got married, and we decided to try – *let's do it, let's have this kid* – and then it happened on the first try.

Now I had been on anti-depressives for a couple years by that point. People get really concerned about taking meds while pregnant, but I stayed on *Sertraline*[47] throughout my pregnancy. I talked about it with my doctor first. We even brought other physicians into the conversation. I'd like to say that I was protective of my pregnancy – but, honestly, I wasn't really attached to what was happening inside of me. If you're pregnant and you don't feel particularly attached to it, please know that it's okay. Some women have always dreamt of being mothers, and that's wonderful, and I'm so glad there are those people in this world – but I wasn't one of them.

I promised brutal honesty, right?

---

[47] Some research has demonstrated links between selective serotonin reuptake inhibitors (SSRIs) and birth defects. However, Sertraline, the SSRI used most often, has not demonstrated this same connection. The CDC reports that although there are increased risks for certain birth defects from SSRIs, the actual risk for a birth defection among babies born to women taking SSRI is still very low.

Yes, I was concerned about my meds affecting my developing child, but I was also thinking about the nine million other things I was having to give up because I was pregnant, and the last thing I needed was to go into a depressive episode. So I stayed on the Sertraline. The problem was, I think the medication veiled a lot of the subtle things that were happening to me. In retrospect, I realize there were signs I just didn't catch on to. Before it got *bad*.

When you get pregnant you have this moment where you're like, *holy shit, this is actually happening.* I remember I had taken a pregnancy test just for fun. I was making coffee one day, and I brought the pregnancy test into the kitchen, looked down at it and saw the second little pink line. I just stopped. Then I turned and poured my coffee down the sink and started making decaf. I called Diego, who was out of town, and told him that I was pulling a wife card. You need to come home. He floored it from San Antonio to Austin, and I told him the news, and we were both super excited together.

But it just doesn't hit you. Your whole world is about to change. It starts with little things. Oh, I don't need to buy tampons because I'm not going to have my period. Yikes, I'm not supposed to drink caffeine. Hey,

I can't unwind with a glass of wine. Oh my God, I'm not supposed to eat sushi, or smoked meats, or soft cheese. All this shit changes and it's not happening to your partner. I didn't realize how frustrating that would be. I remember feeling contentious and telling Diego that I wanted him to go on the pregnancy diet with me for one week. He wouldn't do it. He told me that there was no way anything good would come from both of us being off caffeine. I wanted to shank him in the throat. I got the crazy eyes. He backed away slowly, walked to the fridge, opened the freezer and pulled out some chocolate ice cream; then he put it in front of me with a spoon and walked away. It's like when you're starting to get drunk and you know you're not making smart choices. You can watch yourself doing it and you know that what you're doing doesn't make any sense, but you can't stop yourself.

I remember sitting on the couch next to Diego, just hanging out one day; it was a really nice evening. He was drinking water, respectfully not drinking alcohol in front of me, and I was just staring at the wall. Then I felt the crazy eyes turn on, and I started shaking with rage. I turned to Diego and said, 'I am so angry at you right now.' He was reading a magazine. I remember he stopped, and he didn't make eye contact with me at all. 'And do you know why?' he asked. I said, 'No ... but I am pissed.' He slowly put his magazine down, still not making eye contact. 'Do you want to talk about it?' he asked. I said, 'Don't you mock me!' I wanted to choke him. But as suddenly as it came on, it was gone, and I asked him what he wanted to do for dinner.

I was experiencing big mood swings. Sometimes I felt excited and sad at the same time; I felt guilty about feeling sad, because I was pregnant, and I was married to a wonderful man, and so many great things were happening in my life. I thought I would look like a gargoyle when I was pregnant, because that's how I always pictured pregnant women – or like that scene from *Alien*[48] – but I was actually an adorable pregnant woman. I had that whole glow thing going on. Sure, I had a huge belly, but it was a pretty easy pregnancy overall.

I was accepted into a Master of Biomedical Science program at a medical school and I couldn't believe it was finally happening. Diego and I picked up and moved halfway across the country. He got a position with the Red Cross and had to travel forty-five

---

[48] *Alien* is an American horror and science fiction movie created in 1979, that has also generated numerous sequels. This film won an Academy Award in 1980 for Best Effects, and also nominated for Best Art Direction – Set direction.

minutes each way to work, and so I was alone a lot. At school, I felt really ostracized; it felt as though the women in my class viewed pregnancy as this contagious thing. And I was struggling academically. *Pregnancy brain*[49] is real. Everything gets foggy. You can't remember things well.

Ellison was born two weeks premature. He was a meconium[50] birth, the big scare being that the baby might aspirate some of it. But I was so busy cursing during the birth that I didn't know when Ellison actually popped out. Before I even realized what had happened, a nurse threw him on my chest – it felt like this weird squid – and all of a sudden he was taken away. I kept asking, 'Where is my child? Where is my child?' because you hear how important it is to hold your baby to your chest. But Ellison wasn't breathing. His Apgar score[51], which is a measure of the newborn's

---

[49] While much remains unknown about the brain changes due to pregnancy, one study found that pregnant mothers experienced a reduction in gray matter, most specifically in the frontal and temporal lobe regions. The impacts of this brain loss are not fully understood, but it is thought that these brain changes help create new deeper bonds between the mother and child. The same research study was unable to find memory changes during pregnancy.

[50] Meconium is the early feces (stool) passed by a newborn soon after birth. In some cases, the baby can pass meconium while still inside the uterus. It is possible that babies can aspirate, or swallow, meconium, leading to breathing problems.

[51] Apgar is a quick test performed on a baby at 1 and 5 minutes after birth. The 1-minute score determines how well the baby tolerated the birthing process. The 5-minute score tells the healthcare provider how

health, was like four out of ten, which is not good. And I was so confused. I kept asking, 'Where the hell is my kid?' and I started to feel that his troubled birth was my fault.

As a mother – and I don't know if dads experience the same thing – you can never get away from a sense of guilt. Even if you're doing everything everyone tells you that you're supposed to be doing, you still feel this terrible guilt. I'm not spending enough time with my child. I'm not teaching my child the right things. I'm not being attentive enough. I'm not being loving enough. It's a tremendous amount of pressure being a parent, and I felt that guilt immediately upon Ellison's birth. Why am I not skin-to-skin with my child like I'm supposed to be? But then I finally got to hold him. I had been calling him Sprout throughout the pregnancy because I hadn't been able to humanize him yet. And so I said, 'Hey Sprout,' and he kind of looked at me. I thought I would feel this great love and affection, because this is your child – you've been carrying this thing inside of your body for nine months – but I didn't feel that at all. I felt like, okay, now what? Nobody ever fesses up to that.

---

well the baby is doing outside the mother's womb. A healthcare profession examines the baby's breathing effort, heart rate, muscle tone, reflexes and skin color.

We stayed in the hospital overnight; the next day we took our baby home, and it was just surreal. I felt like any day his real parents were going to show up to pick him up. It felt like I had been babysitting for a really long time, or that we had a really demanding houseguest. A couple days after you deliver, you experience this huge hormonal surge. I remember I was upstairs, and I had to call Diego on the phone because I was bawling uncontrollably. I was convinced he was going to die, and then that they were both going to die, and it was going to happen in a car accident, and it was going to be on a freeway where there were lots of trees. I was convinced that I was going to be alone. I was inconsolable.

My mom, who is a lactation consultant, told me how wonderful breast-feeding is and what a bonding experience it would be. I think I had one session where I thought, *oh, it's cute*; the rest of the time it was like, *kid would you hurry the hell up*. Ellison was a snacker. He would take a few slurps and then smack his lips. But I needed to get to sleep because I had class in the morning. I remember feeling very begrudging. This was supposed to be a nice experience. I was supposed to be enjoying this. But I resented him. I felt stressed. I was sleep deprived. I think a lot of the frustration I felt was because of that. There was depression too. And then the anger came back. I would get so mad because Ellison wouldn't stop crying. Within a week of the birth, he wasn't gaining weight; in fact, he was losing weight. He had intestinal issues because I wasn't producing enough milk, but I didn't want to give him formula because, with my mother being a lactation consultant, I felt like it was rat poison – which it's not – so I'd be sitting there trying to breastfeed him. There were times when I literally wanted to throw him out the window, slam it shut, and just go to sleep. I hated him. And I hated my husband because my whole world was turned upside-down while his was still semi the same. I was just so filled with anger. And I felt so isolated.

It never crossed my mind that it might be a postpartum episode[52].

I guess I should have caught on, or somebody should have caught on, but our family didn't live near us. We were on the other side of the country. And I didn't know my classmates well at all. I remember one

---

[52] Postpartum depression may be mistaken for baby blues at first. Baby blues are emotional, appetite, and sleep problems that last a few days to weeks after a baby is born. Postpartum depression symptoms are more intense and last much longer. They can interfere with a mother's ability to care for a baby and handle other daily tasks. Symptoms can also include difficulty bonding with the baby, withdrawing from friends and family, and radical mood changes.

night just screaming, at the baby, at my husband – 'I have to do school! How am I expected to do anything if I'm not sleeping! I can't handle this! This is bullshit! I didn't even want this kid!' I feel ashamed for saying it, but it's true. Then one day Diego found me crying hysterically in a pile of dirty laundry in the bathroom. I was despondent. *Nothing good is ever going to happen to me. I am never going to get into real medical school. I'm a loser. This child ruined our marriage, ruined my life, and now I have to care for this fucking thing. And I hate it! My body doesn't work the same. Sex is never going to be same. I'm never going to be attractive again.* Everything became so dark.

I didn't know what I was getting into. I didn't know how to handle having a baby. None of my friends had babies. The school made me sit for midterms four days after I gave birth. It was ridiculous. I ended up leaving without finishing the semester, and we moved back to my hometown of Yakima. That was where I experienced the full breakdown.

I had been having little waves of symptoms that I didn't recognize. The anger. The resentment I felt toward Diego and Ellison. I had to leave school and give up my dream to give Diego what he wanted. Off he goes to work every day and here I am stuck taking care of the baby.

When Ellison was six months old, I decided to build a fence for my parents. I wanted to do it as a gift. They had been so supportive of me. I was working on this fence when the neighbor, the husband, comes outside. I remember I started joking with him that I didn't know what I was doing, but I was just trying to make him feel less emasculated; I've done plenty of projects and renovations. But that husband and wife, they seemed to think I didn't know what I was doing. They were telling me how much they cared about how the fence turned out, even though they hadn't contributed a dime into it. Then they started taking down all of my work and building it over again.

I lost my shit. I finally just cracked.

The wife was outside drinking a beer with one of her friends. I was so angry. I wanted to bash her over the head. I started screaming at her. I lost my mind. I threw a two-by-four at her. I took a circle saw and started cutting down the fence. My mom was crying, 'This isn't you! What's going on?' But the world was numb to me. I think it needed to happen. I was just so overwhelmed with life. In the aftermath, people started asking if I had ever experienced postpartum depression. 'No, I'm a good mom,' I said. 'I do what I'm supposed to do.' But that isn't the point at all.

I really wish I had known more of what was happening to me. I felt really duped. Even if I knew it wouldn't be picture-perfect, I had no idea how isolating it would be. I didn't know it could hit you so hard. Parenthood is supposed to be so wonderful. I had no idea what the signs were. I didn't know to reach out. And I'm surprised that nobody realized what was happening to me. I guess it just doesn't cross people's minds. Nobody in obstetrics really talks about postpartum depression at follow-up appointments. You just fill out a questionnaire that asks if you are anxious or depressed. I wish somebody had sat down with me and told me that being a first-time mother is freaking hard. I wish someone had validated all the feelings I thought I shouldn't be having. I wish someone had told me that it's okay to feel this way, and if you are feeling this way, tell us so that we can get you the help that you need. Because this isn't going to last forever. Everything in your world has just changed. Your body has changed. Your priorities have changed. You now have a human being that you are responsible for, and babies need their mothers more than they need their fathers. If you're nursing, you're going to have to get up three times a night; you might hate your partner because he gets to keep on sleeping. Mothers feel a visceral pain when we hear our baby crying. It physically hurts almost. Diego could sleep right through that, but I couldn't. I really wish someone had told me these things.

The fact that I had depression prior to my pregnancy actually made me a higher risk candidate for postpartum. I would have thought it the opposite. I was already taking medication. My depression was controlled. Why would it get worse? This was supposed to be a beautiful time in my life, with my new baby, and my husband – hey, we made this together – but instead I really resented my child.

If other mothers feel similarly, they don't talk about it.

What I would say to a woman who is either pregnant or has just given birth, and maybe she's having some of the same feelings that I had – and I'm not making a mockery of this – but I would tell her that babies suck. They can be little assholes. It's okay to not like them. It's okay to feel like crap, to feel out of control; everything you're feeling is okay. It's not your fault. This is normal. And, be careful, because *mom-shaming* is a real thing. Other mothers will make you feel terrible. People will judge you. Please understand that you can only do the best that you can do. Your feelings are normal. Reach out for help. It might not necessarily be your obstetrician. I'm not sure who the best source is – maybe a friend, or a family member. Call your primary care physician, tell them you need to talk to somebody about depression medication. This doesn't have to be the best time in your life, but it shouldn't be so miserable.

We have a lot of young mothers in our first-year class, so we made a group called *Keepers of Tiny Humans*. I don't know how we all found the time to get away, but we went out to lunch one day. I realized that we have a lot in common. Most of us aren't those types of women who just couldn't wait to become mothers. It was really nice to find a group of students struggling with the same monster. If you're struggling too, don't feel that you're a failure. Society can be really hard on mothers. If you're a mom and you're under pressure – whether it's school, or a job, or just a mother-in-law you don't get along with – recognize that you're not alone. The stress you're going through is not easy. Find your people. Find someone who will be there with you, someone who will listen. It can be life-changing.

# LAURA

*I can't go to medical school. Those people are so smart. I'm just not smart enough. – It's all the crap you tell yourself that holds you back.*

***Generalized Anxiety Disorder***
***Major Depressive Disorder***
***Graves' Disease***

I CAN REMEMBER being depressed all the way back in high school – probably even before that, but I didn't have a name for it back then. I have always been very independent, and I still am. I was an only child, so I was used to being on my own a lot. And I can remember having thoughts of death when I was really young, thoughts about my own death, and death in general, and what does it all mean? I can even remember thinking to myself that other kids probably don't think the way that I do.

I would stare out the window during car trips and look at the little houses going by and I would wonder about the people who lived there. I would think how they will probably die in that house. These were unhappy thoughts for a little kid. And my family, we moved quite a bit. We didn't move quite as often as military families, but I had to start over lots of times. It was hard for me in high school, because that's when kids start to solidify groups of friends, and I moved across the country from Indiana to Utah between my freshman and sophomore years. I did well in school, but it was difficult for me socially. I would wear the 'happy face' all the time, faking it, of course, but making sure that people thought I was a happy, bubbly person. I didn't want anyone to think that anything was wrong with me. I became really good at wearing that face. And I never talked about it with anyone.

I did meet some great people in Utah, but it's difficult when all your friends have siblings and you're all by yourself. I didn't really have a support system. It just wasn't there for me. Sure, I had my parents, but I didn't want them worrying about me. I wanted to be independent. Hey, man, I'm an adult now. I'm fifteen. I've got my learner's permit!

I got my first car sometime after I turned sixteen. I remember driving to school, and there were these hills at the Benches of the Wasatch Valley. I remember wanting to just shift the wheel. It was such a strong urge. Just shift the wheel a little bit and go off the road. It would be so easy.

It really scared me.

God, I'm such a weirdo, I thought. What the hell is wrong with me? I didn't tell anyone. I didn't tell a soul about my thoughts. And it wasn't until way later that I started seeing a therapist, and only after things had gotten so bad that I didn't know what else to do. I had become really good at hiding the things about myself that I didn't want people to know.

After I graduated from high school in Utah, I moved back to Indiana. I attended Indiana University. And it wasn't depression that I experienced so much in college, but anxiety. A fear of failure. I felt it all the time. This sense of inadequacy. I suppose the depression was always present, but not necessarily better or worse. I did some underage drinking, but who doesn't; and when I moved off campus, we had some pretty raging parties, which was great, but I wasn't abusing alcohol. I was a pretty good girl overall.

Now, something about me: when I wanted to do something, I did it. Even if I failed, I was okay with that because I tried. I kept going. And something I decided I wanted to do was to move out to L.A. and get a job working in television. I wanted to do it. So after college, I worked and saved up a little money, and then I moved to L.A. I stayed with a friend who was living out there. She was new to the television industry, working with producers, and then I just fell into a job. It really is a who-you-know kind of thing. I met a fellow alumnus from Indiana University who told me about a position as third production-assistant on a show. 'You want to come do it?'

Sure!

So I started working on a couple of shows on Fox Network[53]. One was called *Oliver Beene*. It had kind of *A Wonder Years*[54] sort of feel. Then I worked on a show called *Cracking Up* that was cancelled. I met a lot of great people and I loved being there, but I was working horrible hours, fifteen-hour days, call-sheets in the early mornings, late script write-ups and alterations,

---

[53] Fox Network (Fox Broadcasting Company) is an American television broadcasting company founded in 1986 by media magnate Rupert Murdoch. It is a subsidiary of the media conglomerate 21st Century Fox. Its headquarters are in Beverly Hills, CA.

[54] The series depicts the social and family life of a boy in a typical American suburban middle–class family from 1968 – 1973, covering ages 12 through 17. Storylines are told through the main character's reflections as an adult in his mid–30s.

and then they'd have new pages for me to deliver at night. So I'd get in my car and drive around L.A. with a stupid map delivering script pages. This was in the days pre-GPS and pre-smartphone. But it was exciting. I was barely twenty years old and working in television like I had dreamt of doing. On the weekends, I would crash hard. I made some great friends out there, but I never talked to anyone about my personal issues: lack of sleep; insomnia; panic attacks.

I was in an awful relationship at that time. You know, I wish therapy was a class you had to take in high school. I feel like every person could benefit from some amount of talk-therapy. Hell, they don't even teach you how to balance a checkbook in high school, let alone how to balance your moods. I didn't know how to handle being in an awful relationship. Have you heard the term *gaslighting?*[55] That's what was happening to me. My relationship was crashing and burning my self-esteem. It took me finally getting away to realize how bad it had gotten, and it's still hard for

---

[55] The concept of *gaslighting* comes to us from Patrick Hamilton's 1938 play, *Gas Light*, known in America as *Angel Street*. Together with his earlier play *Rope,* which was made into a film by Alfred Hitchcock, *Gaslight* tells the story of a man intent on convincing his wife she's insane, in order that he might lay hands on some jewels she has inherited. Gaslighting is a form of psychological manipulation that seeks to sow seeds of doubt in a person making them question their own sanity.

me to think about it. He was so conniving, so manipulative, and I just didn't see it.

Shit finally hit the fan, something in me clicked and I said, *fuck this!* And so at the end of my three-plus year career in television, there was a writers' strike, and I was working part-time at a couple different places when I found a full-time job in an unrelated field. By then most of my friends were beginning to settle down and start families, move to Portland, and I was realizing that this whole television thing wasn't really working out. What am I doing with my life? Then the breakup happened. On top of everything else, my mother wasn't doing well. I realized I had to turn my life around and start over, so I left L.A., moved back to Indiana.

Maybe it was having a different structure in my life, but things were getting better. I had switched majors a lot in college, but my first major had been psychology and I had loved it. I really enjoyed the science. So I thought that I would go back to school. I didn't know what I wanted to do, but I started taking classes on the side, and around this time I entered into another relationship. It was really short – the *rebound* – but it made me realize how toxic my prior relationship had been. I also realized that I had a lot of work to do.

There were a lot of things I still needed to figure out about myself.

I was still in the midst of depression, and I was still anxious, horribly anxious. I fell to the lowest weight I had ever been before. I just stopped eating. I was working out a lot. I realize now that I had an undiagnosed eating disorder. It was a control thing. What do I have control over? –the things I put in my mouth –whether I go to the gym. And so I wasn't in the best health, and I probably wasn't in the best place mentally. I read a lot of self-help books. I became a self-help fanatic. Much of that helped me decide what I wanted to do with my life, because there was always an underlying theme of: *what does it all mean?* I think most people experience that kind of crisis at some point in life.

And then there was the Graves' disease[56].

---

[56] Graves' disease (GD). GD is an autoimmune thyroid disorder characterized by circulating antibodies that stimulate the TSH receptor resulting in hyperthyroidism. GD is a common disorder affecting 0.5% to 1.2% of the population. There is a female-to-male ratio of 5-10:1. Untreated hyperthyroidism can lead to osteoporosis, atrial fibrillation, cardiomyopathy, and congestive heart failure; thyrotoxicosis (thyroid storm) has an associated mortality rate of 20% to 50%.

I was diagnosed with it, and so I did a shitload of research and learned all about Graves'. Basically, it is an autoimmune disorder where your body attacks your thyroid gland. I wonder how long I had Graves' before I was actually diagnosed. It's a kind of disease that doesn't necessarily come on right away. If I had been having issues, I just didn't know. A lot of the symptoms are really non-specific, like weight-loss, anxiety, high heart rate, and depression is also a possible side effect. So it's very chicken and egg; which one came first? And I was poor – I didn't have health insurance; I didn't get blood work done. I had no idea that I had an autoimmune disorder.

Then my mother died. She had long-term diabetes, smoked her whole life – every risk factor that we discuss in medical school. And so although her passing wasn't expected, it also wasn't shocking.

I met a guy and he was so normal, and our relationship was great. It wasn't so up-and-down, and then down-and-down. We dated for a while, and then got engaged. Now he's my husband.

I was working in Toledo, Ohio – just over the line from Indiana – and one day I decided to donate blood at a blood drive. I was told they couldn't take my blood because my blood pressure was too high. And I felt so stressed, always stressed. Have you ever had so much caffeine that your eyeballs shake? That's kind of what it felt like. My body was tingling all the time. And I was tired all the time, but I couldn't sleep. It's just grief. It's just stress. It's this. It's that. I didn't want to put a name to it, but when I was told they couldn't take my blood, I remember crying. I started bawling. What the fuck is wrong with me?! I was getting weaker. I couldn't make it up stairs anymore. My legs felt too weak under me. It felt like I was dying.

I wrote about this in my personal statement when I was applying to medical school. I finally made an appointment to see a doctor, my primary care doctor, and she changed my life. I sat down and talked with her. She hugged me. Suddenly everything let go and I began sobbing. She performed a physical exam and found a giant goiter[57] on my neck. I had no idea it was even there. I couldn't see it. And then she sent me for thyroid tests, and I was diagnosed with Graves' disease.

---

[57] *Goiter* refers to an enlarged thyroid gland. Biosynthetic defects, iodine deficiency, autoimmune disease, and nodular diseases can each lead to goiter, although by different mechanisms. Biosynthetic defects and iodine deficiency are associated with reduced efficiency of thyroid hormone synthesis, leading to increased thyroid-stimulating hormone (TSH), which stimulates thyroid growth as a compensatory mechanism to overcome the block in hormone synthesis.

I was immediately prescribed a beta-blocker[58] to slow down my heart.

I thought it was going to be a mental health issue. I thought she would put me on *Paxil*[59] or some anti-anxiety medication. And she did – she prescribed me *Ativan*[60], as-needed; but after the beta-blocker, I just didn't need it as much as I thought I would.

It's a very osteopathic mindset: the interconnectedness of mind, body, and spirit. Your body influences your mind, and your mind influences your spirit, which is everything. So once the physical

---

[58] Beta blockers, also known as beta-adrenergic blocking agents, are medications that reduce your blood pressure. Beta blockers work by blocking the effects of the hormone epinephrine, also known as adrenaline. When you take beta blockers, your heart beats more slowly and with less force, thereby reducing blood pressure. Beta blockers also help blood vessels open up to improve blood flow.

[59] Paroxetine (Paxil) is used to treat depression, panic attacks, obsessive-compulsive disorder (OCD), anxiety disorders, and post-traumatic stress disorder. It works by helping to restore the balance of a certain natural substance (serotonin) in the brain. Paroxetine is known as a selective serotonin reuptake inhibitor (SSRI). This medication may improve your mood, sleep, appetite, and energy level and may help restore your interest in daily living. It may decrease fear, anxiety, unwanted thoughts, and the number of panic attacks. It may also reduce the urge to perform repeated tasks (compulsions such as hand-washing, counting, and checking) that interfere with daily living.

[60] Lorazepam (Ativan) is a medication used to treat anxiety. Lorazepam belongs to a class of drugs known as benzodiazepines which act on the brain and nerves (central nervous system) to produce a calming effect. This drug works by enhancing the effects of a certain natural chemical in the body (GABA).

part of me was kind of taken care of, I was left with all the mental challenges. Okay, so this is fixed, but why do I still feel like shit? Why do I still feel like an awful failure? I have all these good things going in my life, and I feel like a failure. Why don't I want to get out of bed? What's wrong with me?

I was seeing a few different doctors because of the Graves', but it was my endocrinologist who suggested I see a psychiatrist. Unfortunately, before I had the chance to see a psychiatrist, my husband and I moved rather abruptly to Washington State, and moving is one of the most stressful things a person can do. I started working in the healthcare field. I loved the idea of medical school, but I had really low self-esteem. I can't go to medical school. Those people are so smart. I'm just not smart enough. It's all the crap you tell yourself that holds you back, because I had proven to myself over and over again that when I wanted to do something, I did it; and if I failed, it was fine – I'd find something else.

By this point, I had self-diagnosed myself with depression. I was sure I met the SIG E CAPS score[61].

---

[61] SIG E CAPS: Major Depressive Disorder Diagnostic Criteria -
At least 5 of the following must be present for at least 2 weeks:
Sleep – increased or decreased (if decreased, often early morning awakening)
Interest – decreased

And I accepted it. It wasn't just the medical diagnosis of having Graves' disease – I really needed to talk to someone. I hadn't been processing my grief. And so one day I actually wrote everything down, because, being manic, when you have that 'high,' you get all these great ideas. I remember thinking that I needed to write down all my thoughts and feelings before I became too fogged to remember – because when I go to the doctor and they ask me 'how are you doing today?' and I answer 'I'm fine' ... I can't do that anymore. I made a conscious decision right then that I was going to figure myself out, and I started by writing out my feelings. I wrote about my mom. I wrote about my relationships. I wrote about my life and my struggles. And when I answered all those questions at the doctor's office, I answered them sincerely. She determined that, yes, I do indeed have major depressive disorder.

I remember thinking – *Well duh!*

It was time to fix this. I couldn't keep going on like this. I had to do something. I don't have a really dramatic story where I was ready to just end it all or

---

**G**uilt/worthlessness
**E**nergy – decreased or fatigued
**C**oncentration/difficulty making decisions
**A**ppetite and/or weight increase or decrease
**P**sychomotor activity – increased or decreased
**S**uicidal ideation

anything like that. Yes, I'd had suicidal thoughts – but I think most people do at some point in their life. What if tomorrow I just didn't exist? Maybe I'm being naïve, but I think like everyone sort of faces that question at some point. For me, I knew that I was thinking about it a lot more frequently than I should have been. My physical diagnosis was beginning to be controlled and I was left with all the mental crap that I needed to process and deal with.

I was prescribed the first line therapy of *Celexa*[62]. It's a SSRI, pretty well tolerated in most people, and fairly cheap. But medications often take time before they start having an effect, and my primary care doctor understood that I needed talk therapy as well as the pharmacotherapy, and that she wasn't comfortable managing my long-term mental health. She referred me to a psychiatrist as well as a psychologist. I enjoyed the psychologist – the psychiatrist not so much.

I simply didn't have a baseline to know what bad psychiatry was. I should have realized when I started crying in his office and he just crossed his arms

---

[62] Celexa (trade), Citalopram (generic). Citalopram is used to treat depression. It may improve your energy level and feelings of well-being. Citalopram is known as a selective serotonin reuptake inhibitor (SSRI). This medication works by helping to restore the balance of a certain natural substance (serotonin) in the brain.

and looked at me. I felt like a piece of shit on his shoe. Why am I here? This was a mistake. And maybe I'm looking at it through a different lens now that I'm an osteopathic medical student, but this man was a D.O. It really upsets me. I suppose, however, that there are shitty doctors in every field and in every capacity. That's part of the reason I decided to go into medicine. That decision came late in my life.

I had insurance at the time, and I don't know what I would have done if I hadn't had good insurance. I don't think I would have had the money to pay for both medication *and* therapy. Even with my co-pay, it was still pretty expensive. I was basically going to therapy every other week. But I did love my therapist. A lot of people don't luck out with their therapist like I did. I don't see her anymore. I guess I maxed out with her. I remember making the call and saying, 'I don't think I need to see you anymore,' and it felt in a weird way like a breakup. Of course, she's a professional. She was fine with it. It's what is supposed to happen. You're supposed to take the tools they teach you, use them, and then check in after you sort through your shit. But now that I'm in medical school, it's like, holy Jesus, I need therapy more now than ever. But who can find the time? It's my weakness right now. A lot of people think that once therapy is over, then you're done. I'm fixed. But it's not like that. We are such works in progress, and that's life, and there is always going to be something else. Even when you have all the tools, sometimes you just don't know how to use them. Or maybe you need to learn a different way of using them. I still deal with my fear of failure. I still need guidance, and that's okay.

Now, here I am in medical school, and I've realized that Imposter Syndrome[63] is a real thing. *They made a mistake. I don't belong here. Someone will eventually find out that I'm not supposed to be here.* Yes, this first year has been really difficult. A lot of emotions have surfaced that I haven't dealt with in a long time. I knew coming in that it was going to be hard. And being around all these young folks here at school has been really invigorating, but it has also been really challenging. Everyone has their own little cliques, and I just never really clicked with anyone. I get along with people well, but I never really found a solid friend group. I have my husband, of course, but he doesn't live with me. He's back home in Spokane. We're three hours apart from each other.

---

[63] Imposter Syndrome refers to a psychological phenomenon in which people are unable to internalize their accomplishments. This syndrome is characterized as a persistent and internalized fear of being exposed as a fraud. The term was coined by clinical psychologist Pauline Clance and Suzanne Imes in 1978.

So this first year is kind of wrapping up, and I've been going on autopilot for a while now – just trying to stay above water. It's really easy to let it all go, forget all the good habits you've learned, put everything else on the back-burner and focus your everything on school, because this is a very expensive investment that we have going on. There's a lot at stake. Passing anatomy is just more important right now. And I want to do well. I want to do well for my future patients. But, you know, you have to put your own oxygen mask on first or you're not going to be much help to the person sitting beside you.

I'm trying to be a lot more open minded these days. I'm trying to consider what other people are experiencing. It's easy to pass judgment. Like my old psychiatrist, that man who I thought was terrible, I wonder what he was going through? –maybe he was burnt out –maybe he wasn't taking care of his own emotional health –maybe he is a perfect therapist for someone else and just didn't fit what I needed. I'm trying to be open to more perspectives than simply my own. Because we become so wrapped up in how *we're* doing all the time that it makes it easy to overlook how others are doing. And I want to be okay with others. I want to be accepting.

We're not going to have all the answers. As future doctors, we're just not going to have all the answers. I think of all the information that I've forgotten from first-semester anatomy, and it scares the crap out of me. Oh my God, we have a final exam in like two weeks ... over *everything*! Our professors, unless they do this every day – which they do – they'd forget what exact sensory nerve innervates the receptor of the left lower whatever. I suppose we'll just get better over time, but we can't be expected to know *everything*. We shouldn't put ourselves under that kind of pressure. We need to take care of ourselves. We need to help ourselves. And we can't overlook the people in our lives who love us and matter to us most.

My husband – he's my main support. I should thank him for putting up with me, [64] but it's so easy to get wrapped up in the day-to-day stress of medical school. I'm sure other people have just as stressful an existence as we do too. It's just a different perspective is all.

So, yes, there are many mental health illnesses that will never be cured. They're diseases, like diabetes,

---

[64] Thanks honey. I treat you like shit. Thanks for not leaving me.

and you can't cure diabetes. My Graves' disease, although it's not a mental health disorder, it's just as much a struggle now as it was at the beginning. Your thyroid, unless you have it surgically removed, thyroid hormone blood levels don't just go away overnight. I have to constantly get blood work done to assess where it needs to be. And even though I don't have a functioning thyroid, there's still some tissue there. You can still feel it when you palpate my neck. It just doesn't produce as much hormone on a daily basis, so I supplement it with *Synthroid*[65]. I'll be on this medication for the rest of my life. I'll die if I don't take it. It might take a while, but the body requires thyroid hormone for metabolism. It used to be that I struggled with *hyper*-thyroidism; but now, after having ionizing radiation in my mid-twenties to destroy my thyroid gland, I deal with *hypo*-thyroidism. I've shifted from one end of the spectrum to the other.

I guess I feel like a bloody hot mess with all these things going on in me. Of course, a person is more than just a disease or a bunch of symptoms. There

---

[65] Levothyroxine is used to treat an underactive thyroid (hypothyroidism). It replaces or provides more thyroid hormone, which is normally produced by the thyroid gland. Low thyroid hormone levels can occur naturally or when the thyroid gland is injured by radiation/medications or removed by surgery. Having enough thyroid hormone is important for maintaining normal mental and physical activity. In children, having enough thyroid hormone is important for normal mental and physical development.

is a whole plethora of things happening in a person's life that influences the body, and then the mind, and then the spirit. And so what influences what first? Did I have Graves' disease first? Did I always have depression? I don't know. But I ignored my issues for way too long. I'm a stubborn bitch. I'm way too independent. I've always been this way. When I was a little girl, I only wanted to dress myself. I'm going to do it *my* way and nobody's going to help me.

Well, *fuck that!*

We *need* people to help us. Honestly, everyone out there, if you are struggling in any way, *please* do not be afraid to go and talk to somebody. Do *not* hold it in as long as I did. I could have kept holding it in, and God knows ... I wouldn't be in medical school right now, that's for sure, and I probably wouldn't be married. I might have done something stupid. So if there's anything you take away from this, *please* don't be afraid to ask for help. You're *not* going to fix it yourself. That's just not how it works. It's not something you can isolate and deal with yourself. And I waited way too long. If I had gotten help sooner, I probably would have been a doctor by now, and I probably would have gotten my pilot's license already – which is another thing on my horizon – because, honestly, I would have become a better version of myself sooner.

I'm going to be honest with you right now – I actually stopped taking my medication. I tapered myself off, partly because of the requirements for pilot licensure. The regulations are complicated regarding pilots with behavioral health issues. They are usually approved on a case-by-case basis. And I understand why – they don't want you keeling over during a flight – but it's very archaic. If you're on *Lisinopril*[66] for high blood pressure, or on a heart medication, you might not be approved. I hope that as future physicians we can help change the current perspective on mental health.

I watched a movie a few weeks ago that I remember having watched as a kid. It was about a girl with schizophrenia, and it kind of infuriated me because I realized that we really haven't progressed all that much medically, and it's been like thirty years. But I can say that the subject of mental health is becoming more approachable. People aren't like, oh my God, what the hell is that? It's more like, oh how interesting,

---

[66] Lisinopril is used to treat high blood pressure, which can help prevent strokes, heart attacks, and kidney problems. It can also be used to treat heart failure and to improve survival after heart attack. Lisinopril belongs to the drug class ACE inhibitors, and works by relaxing blood vessels.

tell me more, how are you dealing with that? People seem to have a more of a global perspective today, and we are becoming less afraid of behavioral health.

It was a very big epiphany realizing that I'm not alone in my struggles. I'm in a position today where I might be the one to help others move forward. Because I was there. I made it through. You're going to make it through too. We're going to keep moving forward, because this is the only direction we have, and because we can't stand still. We have to keep going.

# T E D

*I think the biggest thing is not to fight it. If I'm not focusing, then I accept that. Okay, I'm not focusing right now ... So I'll go and do something. Something to take my mind off of it. Then I'll try again.*

## *Attention Deficit Hyperactivity Disorder*

I WAS A MEMBER of an outdoor education and leadership cohort in the honors college at the University of Utah. All of us in the cohort lived together, and every Friday it was compulsory that we went out and did something. We'd go on a climb, or a hike, and often our professors would join us. At the beginning of the year, there was a four-day rafting trip for us to get to know each other. During that same rafting trip of my second year, I was a mentor for the incoming freshman, and our professors decided to conduct research on *Attention Restoration Theory*.

\* \* \*

I have ADHD. I didn't learn this until my junior year of college, just two years ago. I was getting ready to take the MCAT and I was being tested for dyslexia – I'm also dyslexic by the way. I was trying to get accommodations for taking the MCAT, and the doctor I was seeing told me that the testing administration is really kind of stingy on providing accommodations for students with dyslexia. It's really frustrating, and it's something that I've dealt with for a long time. I tried to get accommodations in high school for the ACT. I had documentation from a physician saying that I was dyslexic, but all I would ever hear back was, 'Well, you have good grades so it can't be hurting you that much.' But then the doctor who was testing my dyslexia noticed that I showed signs of ADHD. He told me that testing administrations are more willing to give accommodations for students with ADHD, much more than for dyslexia, so let's try that route.

About six months after I was diagnosed with ADHD, I decided to try taking *Adderall*[67]. I took the

---

[67] This combination medication is used to treat attention deficit hyperactivity disorder. It works by changing the amounts of certain natural substances in the brain. Amphetamine/dextroamphetamine belongs to a class of drugs known as stimulants. It can help increase your ability to pay attention, stay focused on an activity, and control behavior problems. It may also help you to organize your tasks and improve listening skills. This drug is also used to treat a certain sleeping disorder (narcolepsy) to help you stay awake during the day. It should not be used to treat tiredness or to hold off sleep in people who do not have a sleep disorder.

twelve-hour release tablets and didn't like how it made me feel. Everyone always thinks it's weird when I say this, but Adderall made me feel really ... happy. What's wrong with being happy? Nothing, except that I would feel when it would wear off. It was like I would fall off of it. And then I just didn't like that it was altering how I was feeling. It definitely helped me focus though. I just didn't like the side effects.

I know I didn't really give the meds as much of a shot as I should have. But I was prescribed them about two months before I was scheduled to take the MCAT, and I didn't want to change my study approach at that point. Then it was my senior year of college, and I had already been accepted into medical school, so I didn't really want to start trying meds again. I'm open to them though. I don't have any stigma against medication. I think whatever you can do that works for you, so that you're well controlled, is what you should do.

I have a really hectic work flow. I tend to study for ten minutes and then watch twenty minutes of snowboarding videos, and then I'll kick it into focus again. That's one thing with ADHD that people forget – there's the hyper-focus part of it too. If I can get myself into a mood like that, and it tends to come particularly after I watch snowboarding videos, then I'm better able to get into that hyper-focused state. And then I can get a lot accomplished.

Going outside and doing something active helps get me into that state of hyper-focus even better than watching videos. I don't know if I was doing this before I learned about Attention Restoration Theory; I certainly wasn't doing it on purpose, but I guess it just happened sometimes. I'd find myself thinking, *Oh man, I'm getting a lot done today.* And I wasn't sure if it was because I was so physically exhausted after going on a long hike that all I could do was study, but I definitely noticed a correlation. I just never sought it out intentionally.

Now I come from a very outdoorsy family. All my best memories are of being outside. I just can't recommend it enough. I get out as much as I can. Most years I spend over fifty nights in a tent. I figured it out actually: I bought my tent for two-hundred-fifty bucks, and I'm down to like seventy-five cents a night now. Every time I spend a night in it, I'm saving money, so every chance I get I try to get out. Even now that I'm in medical school. I still probably get out and hike two or three days a week. I find that it really helps my ADHD.

Dr. David Strayer[68], who directed the study on Attention Restoration Theory during that rafting trip I was on – he is currently conducting research comparing the effects on our attention of actually being physically outdoors versus looking at nature photos. Looking at photos is not as significant, of course – but they're using a lot of virtual reality imagery now. There was a guy in England doing research using a three-dimensional room, which is really cool, and he had some good results.

There was a study in a California State Prison too; actually, it wasn't quite as scientific as a study. It was basically a prison weight-lifting room – cement walls, lots of guys yelling, dropping weights, everything you'd imagine – then there was another weight room and on the walls they had video-images of green hills and perfect blue skies with white clouds

---

[68] Dr. David Strayer is a cognitive psychologist at the University of Utah who has investigated the effects of distraction on performance in numerous studies. His research has clearly shown the large cost of common distractions - like cell phone use and texting - on driving performance. Talking on the cell-phone increases the risk of accidents fourfold - the same amount as driving while intoxicated above the legal limit. As he and many other researchers have shown, the act of talking on the phone is the culprit - not holding the phone in one's hand. There is thus no difference between handheld and hands-free phones in cars. Apart from this applied research in human attention, Dr. Strayer has also identified a small set of people who seem to be able to multitask without a significant cost to their performance. Identifying the characteristics of these so-called 'supertaskers' is a new topic he currently pursues.

drifting by. They found that when an inmate would start yelling, other inmates would try to calm him down. It was like they were saying, *Don't ruin this. This is our forty minutes where we get to be 'outside.'* The inmates did a lot better in that second environment.

There was another study held in New York where they found that by merely being within sight of nature – a park just out your window, for instance – at-risk youth experienced increased self-discipline. People living within a half-mile of green space, regardless of whether they actually go to the green space, have decreased risk of depression, anxiety, heart disease, diabetes, asthma, and migraines. There was a panel of fifteen other diseases too. So even if you don't use the green space, it's still beneficial. And look how close we are, here in Central Washington, to miles and miles of apple orchards and cherry orchards. It's no different than being near a park, especially if you're not going to the park. So I feel really lucky to live here and be studying medicine here.

There are similar studies being conducted on this phenomenon in various northern regions – in Alaska, for instance, especially during the winter season when these areas tend to have higher rates of alcoholism and suicide, possibly because of the long stretches of darkness and isolation. Scandinavian nations are doing work into this theory as well.

Attention Restoration Theory basically posits that if you spend time outside you'll be more relaxed, happier, and better able to focus. It sounds grandiose, but this is basically what the different facets of research come down to. It is so simplistic that it's hard to answer against it – but then it's actually almost as hard to argue for it. A lot of people will say, 'Well of course going outside makes you focus more … I guess?' It's easy to be skeptical because it seems too easy, and that's why research backing it up is super important.

There are four properties that must be met within the natural environment for the restoration effect to work:

> *Extent*: the scope to which a person feels immersed in the environment;

> *Being Away*: an escape from the habitual activities of daily life;

*Soft Fascinations*: aspects of the environment that effortlessly capture a person's attention; and

*Compatibility*: a person must want to be exposed to and appreciate the environment.

In my mind, and especially when looking at it from my ADHD-influenced point of view, the *Soft Fascinations* property is the most important of the four pillars. Things in the natural environment just grab your attention. You can become enthralled in the minutia. I think this is what triggers me into a hyper-focused state.

So we had about eighty students on that rafting trip at the University of Utah. I was lucky enough to administer some of the examinations used to determine how well people are in fact restoring their attention. We divided the students into two groups. As one of the researchers, I took one group and administered a test called the Multiple Uses Test. It was a test of creativity, one of the easier cognitive functions to assess. On a sheet of paper was a word, for instance the word 'Hammer.' Under it the volunteer is asked to write down all the things a hammer might be used for. You can use it for hammering nails, use it as a doorstop, use it to scratch your back, to smash spiders, scare away a dog, whatever it may be. The other group was administered a test called the Remote Associates Test. On a sheet of paper there are three words, for example you might see the words 'Belly, Barrel, Root'. The volunteer has to figure out what one word brings the three words together. The answer to this example would be 'Beer'. You can have a *beer belly*, a *beer barrel*, and *root beer*. On the third day of the rafting trip, each group would receive the opposite test.

I've read that Dr. Strayer has more recently taken a portable EEG[69], a functional MRI, into the field. He demonstrated that when assessing volunteers in an urban environment, the brain exhibits greater flow to the amygdala, which processes fear and anxiety. When assessing volunteers in a natural environment, the EEG lit up the anterior geniculate of the insula, which is where empathy and altruism are processed. So there's much more research than just cognitive creativity.

I also read that Korea has embraced this theory so much that they're building a one-hundred million dollar healing complex and planting thirty-four forests.

---

[69] An electroencephalogram (EEG) is a test that detects electrical activity in your brain using small, metal discs (electrodes) attached to your scalp. Brain cells communicate via electrical impulses and are active all the time, even when asleep. An EEG is one of the main diagnostic tests for epilepsy, and can play role in diagnosing other brain disorders.

The forests were supposed to be have been planted by last year, so hopefully they're there now. They set up a train system – they call it *The Happy Train* – to take children who have been bullied into the forest for two days of restorative therapy. Korea is a country known for its demanding work-culture. A survey at Samsung found that seventy percent of its employees described their jobs as causing them depression. But it's also a country taking positive steps, and they are wholeheartedly behind this theory.

There is a national geographic article, *Your Brain on Nature*[70], that is fantastic. It does a really good job of bringing together different research points in a non-technical way. The author, who is from New York, went on a camping trip with Dr. Strayer, and hearing her point of view on Attention Restoration Theory and how she felt the change over her three days of immersion in nature is really interesting.

So if you are not particularly outdoorsy, I would suggest that you start small. Don't go on an exhausting hike; just go to a park and sit down. I don't think you necessarily have to love it immediately. Don't go crazy.

---

[70] "This is Your Brain on Nature" is an article in the January 2016 edition of National Geographic Magazine, available for free on their website.

Don't read *Wild*[71] and think you need to go backpack the Pacific Northwest Trail. There are lots of different things you can do. Watch a nature video. Sure, you're not going to experience the same result, but it might help. Something that I've been wanting to do is to grow a little garden in my house. I'm not sure if this pertains to Attention Restoration Theory, but it's something I've been thinking about. There's minutia that we never notice when just tracing the veins of a leaf.

I'm a medical student who has ADHD and I honestly don't think that it's too much of a detriment. There are so many people who have been diagnosed with it that I'm not embarrassed by it at all. I was about twenty-one when I was diagnosed and when I decided that medication wasn't right for me. Instead, I really try to apply the Attention Restoration Theory into my life. And I certainly care about the research. It's important to me. Unfortunately, I'm garbage at neurology – but I think I can play just as significant a role as an ER physician, or as a surgeon, or whatever field I end up going into, by just speaking out in support of it. If you were just diagnosed with ADHD, depression, bipolar,

---

[71] *Wild: From Lost to Found on the Pacific Crest Trail* - A chronicle of one woman's one thousand one-hundred-mile solo hike undertaken as a way to recover from a recent personal tragedy. Written by Cheryl Strayed in 2012. Movie produced in 2014, directed by Jean-Marc Vallée, and starring Reese Witherspoon.

you name it – maybe you can apply this theory to the management of your own mental illness. And maybe it can help.

I think the biggest thing is not to fight it. If I'm not focusing, then I accept that. Okay, I'm not focusing right now. It won't do me any good to try to study because I'm not retaining anything. So I'll go and do something. Something to take my mind off of it. I might do fifty pushups. Then I'll try again. If I'm still not feeling it, I'll go and try doing something else. Sometimes though you just have to force yourself to study. I am naturally one-hundred percent a procrastinator. That's one reason why deadlines are good for me. When I reach a deadline, it's like, okay, I just need to study no matter what. And then I'm able to forge myself onward.

There's a pond close to my apartment, and I really love redwing blackbirds. I think they're one of the coolest and most underrated birds. They're super common, and they have the most beautiful call. They're very vocal. I go down to the pond, and even if I don't see them, I can hear them. And then I relax. I don't really meditate, but it helps me relax. I bring my notes with me sometimes and try to study, but I'm not sure how I feel about doing that. I don't want to pollute this place. Sitting at that pond and listening to the blackbirds – it's my meditation.

# HEATHER

*There might be confusion. People can be raped by someone they love. You can be raped by your husband, or your wife. It's complicated. I'm not going to sit here and say that as long as you talk about it it's easy.*

***Sexual Assault Survivor***
***Generalized Anxiety Disorder***
***Major Depressive Disorder***
***ADHD***

HONESTLY, I CAN COUNT on one or two hands the number of people I've shared this with, and it's not because I'm not healed – it's just something that doesn't come up. It happened a while ago now, and I've changed so much. When I first told people about the assault, it didn't go over well. I think that contributed to my being so selective in sharing my story. It was a long process of figuring everything out with my therapist. I've worked through so much now. And being in medical school now, I feel so much stronger.

Of course, the word *Victim* is a word a lot of people don't want to identify with. I try to use the word *Survivor*. The whole caveat is that it's different for everyone. Everyone heals differently. We met a woman last semester in our professional development course who had been abducted as a child and sex trafficked for most of her life. She had only really started healing a few years ago, and she's in her forties now. I asked her what the first step toward recovery was, and she said that her first step was speaking in front of people. Within just a few months she went from not even realizing that she had been trafficked for most of her life to speaking in front of groups like our medical class. She said that after she first spoke it aloud, she couldn't function for about a week. But it was her form of therapy. So it's interesting – healing is so different for everyone.

The incident was just a piece of what I had to resolve. I needed to talk about the shame I felt. I imagine that survivors of other sorts of crimes don't experience shame in the same way. While my feelings were valid – *any* feelings are valid after experiencing a trauma – sexual assault isn't something you should feel ashamed of. It's not an inherently shameful thing. For me, I'm not sure if I'd be able to talk about it now were it not for all the years that have passed, and the therapy, and my coming to terms with it.

\* \* \*

I grew up in a beautiful college town in Wisconsin. Depression runs in my family. I started experiencing symptoms early in high school. I was unhappy a lot. I struggled socially. My parents are both primary care physicians and they pushed me to start seeing the same psychiatrist my mother was seeing, and who was covered by our insurance. We didn't connect at all. I was confused. I felt a lot of shame even then – I don't know why shame is such a part of my life. I do want to offer my parents grace for what they did – but I was struggling, and the first thing they jumped to was that I had a diagnosis and that I needed the same medication my mother was taking: *bupropion*[72]. I felt that my parents didn't understand I was still just a kid.

It's a hard balance with teenagers – and I'm passionate about childhood health care and the politics behind it – but we expect teenagers to act like adults and they're not. We don't give them the legal rights to even pretend to be adults. There's a lot going on in their minds. They're still developing. I think we're too quick in determining that a child or teenager needs pharmacological help.

Yet I got better.

---

[72] Bupropion is used to treat depression. It can improve your mood and feelings of well-being. It may work by helping to restore the balance of certain natural chemicals (neurotransmitters) in your brain.

I was put on Bupropion in my sophomore year of high school. I think there were a lot of assumptions made about me in high school, and they were really hurtful. Maybe it's just normal teenager stuff, but I wasn't happy there. I had dreams. And so I decided to graduate early. Most students who graduate early are those who need to help provide for their families, or those who are really struggling in the school environment, but I was just excited to start college. I loved learning. Sure, it was an escape from the little blue-collar town I lived in, but I really did love learning. By the end of my senior year, I was doing better.

I was accepted into both Boston University and University of Wisconsin Madison. My grandparents had gone to Madison. My parents went there. My sister *was* there. I wanted to move across the country and do something totally different. I had these *dreams*, and I was really happy. I was still taking the Bupropion and I felt that my head was in the right place. And so in early January, I packed up and left for Boston. I didn't know anyone.

There were a lot of harsh realizations I had to learn. People made fun of my accent. There are lots of cultural and societal differences on the East Coast.

Much of it seemed to involve who-you-know – an identity based off of name and home and school and where you work – and it has more weight I think on the East. It was a culture shock. But I wanted to stay in Boston. I wanted to get involved in things. I wanted to get to know the city, and people. I was becoming an adult. I had to learn the value of money. I had to figure out how to grocery shop, how to do laundry, all those college things. And this goes back to high school, but I didn't have the tools I needed to make friends, and to keep friends. I think young women often have a hard time with this.

Not having a group of people, and not really knowing how to develop that, really added to my struggle. Even today, my instinct is to depend on myself. I tend to do this instead of seeking help from family or professionals. I'm not sure why either, because I come from a healthy family. I should have more sense than that. But it was certainly a big part of who I was back then.

I really was happy when I first got there. I was enjoying the freedoms of not living under my parent's roof. I moved into the dorms. I was meeting students. I went out to parties.

*I can just tell you ...*

I didn't just go right into the story because, honestly, when somebody says they've been sexually assaulted, there's too often a focus on the trivial things. *Did you know the person? Were you drinking? What were you wearing?* Those things don't matter. It's like – if a pedestrian is walking on the sidewalk, and maybe they've had a few drinks, and then a car hops over the median and crashes into them – you know, they were walking *on the sidewalk*. It doesn't matter if they had been drinking. You're not in the wrong for that. It shouldn't be part of the conversation. I find it mind-boggling that for some reason it is so much of the conversation. You can watch a woman walk down the road and you'll see how a lot of men in this world view women, and how a lot of men view public spaces as these places that women walk into for their pleasure. We're made to feel that we have to present ourselves in a certain way, that we are entering into a zone that is not ours. So the discussion of *what were you wearing?* – I like to keep that out.

I went out with some people to a neighborhood called Allston. The dorms that I lived in were on the corner there. I had made one pretty good friend at this point, but he was out of town visiting his girlfriend at Boston College, so I went out with some people from my dormitory. I knew them by name, but not too well.

It's weird remembering this. I haven't thought about this place in a while.

It wasn't a dark raging basement or anything, but for whatever reason there was a rep from an energy drink company passing out free drinks. After a while, I don't know, but the way I felt, and the things that happened ... I think someone put something in my drink. I've never experienced anything like it. Some of this is memory and some is what I heard from others. I started making out with a guy on a couch in front of everyone. This is not something I would ever do. Then I passed out in his lap. Obviously, I should not have been there.

There was a guy there from my dorm floor who was part of the group that went to the party. I don't think I had ever had a private conversation with him before. I guess I wasn't doing very well, and he must have offered to walk me back to the dormitory. I remember we went out a door, and I thought it would lead outside, but then I realized that we were in a stairwell. He must have led me up the stairs because there was a door at the top and it was closed. In that little space between the top of the stairs and that closed door, he started kissing me. But I wasn't having it. I tried to walk away. I fell down half a flight of stairs. And then I made it clear that I wanted to go home. So he walked me back.

I remember walking into the dormitory and thinking to myself, *Okay Heather, don't look drunk. Get yourself together.* The dorms were super strict about alcohol, and this policy forced students out into the neighborhoods to drink. I thought I was going to my room. The next thing I remember is that I was in *his* room – it was across the hallway and through the lobby – and he was trying to have sex with me. I was mostly passed out. I wasn't really moving. I remember saying *no*. I remember feeling frustrated, and scared. I was on my period, and I knew I was on my period – and I'm saying that because it bothers me when people imply that sexual assault is an excuse that women make when they've had sexual experiences they regret. I had no desire or intention to sleep with this guy. But in that dark room, I was immobile. I only remember bits and pieces of the things he tried. They still come up as triggers. Little things that he was doing.

I woke up in a puddle of my own blood. I pulled my pants on. The button was broken off. My boots were ripped. I felt that horrible shame, the 'walk of shame' as I crossed the lobby back to my room. Then I vomited. I tried to figure out what was happening. There were hickeys all over my neck. A few days later I discovered that a tampon had been shoved inside of me.

My friend who had been away at Boston College that night later asked me, 'Hey, so what happened with what's-his-name? I saw him washing his sheets. Sounds like you guys got dirty. People say they heard you screaming *Fuck me daddy.*'

I was shocked.

The guy was telling people that we had anal sex. I had never had anal sex. I felt that I would have known if it had happened. And 'fuck me daddy' just isn't something I ever would have said. But everyone on my dormitory floor, all my new friends, they thought I was this … I don't know what. Suddenly there were stories that everyone was whispering that were very different from what I had experienced. I didn't know how to deal with it.

I tried telling my friend that it hadn't been consensual. He didn't believe me. And we didn't talk about it after that. I hadn't been able to articulate what had happened to me. I didn't even realize that I had been sexually assaulted. It seems like everybody today is trained on sexual assault, and maybe I had been too, but I just didn't understand it. *Rape* was something that happened in dark alleys. It wasn't something that happened when you were drinking at a party, and not by someone you knew. You know, I'm a smart person, but I just didn't understand what had happened to me. I knew that it sucked. And for a long time after that, every night when I'd try to sleep it would replay over and over again, and I would try to figure out what I did wrong, and what I could have changed.

I never filed a police report, and I never went to a hospital or did a rape-kit. I didn't think I had been assaulted. I thought it was just a horrible night that I regretted. That it might have been a crime wasn't even on my radar. I felt terrible shame. You might have to be a woman to understand this. I'm not saying it to offend men, but only to put context into how we view female sexuality as a double-standard. We don't want a woman who is prudish, but if she sleeps with too many people then she's a slut. I was at a time of my life when I was exploring what casual sex meant to me. Was it something that I even desired? I hadn't engaged in it too much, but I had *some* experience with it, and I think that ties into it. Was this just a casual sex encounter gone wrong? Or is this what casual sex is? I was eighteen years old. I was trying to figure out what these things meant to me.

Unfortunately, I think that sex isn't something we regard for female pleasure. I hadn't quite grasped yet that it *should* be for pleasure, and if it's not pleasurable then something's wrong. I think women are often taught that if it's not pleasurable, then you're doing it wrong – but that's okay, because it's for *him*. I think I internalized that sex wasn't about the woman.

I'm digressing, but this is important – you ask a man, when was it that you realized you were a sexual being? Maybe upon discovering masturbation. But when I first realized that I was a sexual being – and I think a lot of women might identify with this – I was a prepubescent twelve-year old walking my dog down the street when some men started yelling nasty comments at me. A lot of young girls grow up thinking that sex is something that happens *to* them. We're taught that we're here for somebody else's pleasure. Much of it is just built into our society. 'Did you get some?' 'Did you screw her?' It's very rudimentary, but these questions suggest that sex is based around *his* experience, *him* getting something. We're assuming heterosexual dynamics, but if we talk about sex between same-sex couples, it's easier to see that there is more to it than just a man having an orgasm.

Now even then I identified as a feminist. My mom was a feminist. I grew up with strong female role models. Yet I was still living this very typical narrative of a person who doesn't feel in control of sex. I felt that sex was something that was wanted of me, something that I could deliver. It was something that sometimes I may get pleasure from and sometimes I may not. Sometimes it might even bring me great shame. But that's my fault. For being a woman.

That experience did strip me of my identity in many ways. I no longer felt that I could go out and capture the world. It's a character trait that we naturally associate with men. *He just went out and got that job. He went and became an entrepreneur.* But there's so much complexity to it. What allows someone to be that type of person? And in a world that forces us into behaving in certain ways?

I don't think I was sheltered, but I did grow up in a bubble. My parents told me that I could do anything. I could be anything. I had these dreams. But then I was struck with the reality that to be an outgoing woman in this world means that people will take advantage of you, or they will try to strike you down, or they will make assumptions about you. Like those *friends* from my dormitory in Boston. I was an ambitious and outgoing person, and I think they tied the negative of that persona into the sexual assault. *She's just this annoying slut. She's just totally full of herself.* Yes, I was stripped of my identity as the intelligent girl with big dreams who took control of her education and her life. After the assault, I just walked through the world differently.

I couldn't stay in Boston. It was just too expensive. It's one of *the* most expensive schools, probably about the same as what I'm paying for medical school now. So I reapplied to University of Wisconsin Madison and I got in, but I didn't care. I was in a rough place emotionally. My high school friends were still going to school during the day, and I was at home doing nothing. It was a weird summer. I hadn't stayed in touch with them all too well. I was the girl who had gone off with big dreams, and here I was again. *Hey everybody, I'm back. I just went off for a while*. I was really depressed. A trickle of events had made my situation very clear to me. And then there was the suicide attempt. I had been thinking about it for several months. It's scary to talk about even now. This ever-present reality seeps into your being – it's like the sky is blue, your shirt is gray, and the world would be better if you weren't here.

My mom asked again if I wanted to see a therapist. I think I said *no*.

It was a rough summer. I was behaving indifferently. My parents probably thought I was just bummed because of leaving Boston. I didn't leave because of the assault though; I moved because of money. I think my parents saw me as a bitchy teenager instead of a broken person. We didn't have a good relationship. And I didn't have the friends that I had had before.

I went off all my medications when I moved to Madison to start school again. I think I sensed that I needed to change something in my life. It wasn't a smart thing to do. The university required all freshman to live in the dorms, so I had to do the whole dorm thing again, and I didn't want to be there. I couldn't sleep. I was experiencing PTSD[73]-type thoughts at night. I started drinking to help me sleep; sometimes I would stay up as late as I could just to pass out. And I wasn't doing well in my classes – I mean, I was doing okay, but not as well as the students who wanted to go to medical school. Then I stopped advocating for myself. I was very quick to say, *Wow, I'm not one of those Type A students, so med school must not be the thing for me.* This terrible thing had happened to me and I deteriorated into a person who felt things were beyond her control. I was letting life just happen instead of taking charge of it. The driving force of my identity had totally flip-flopped.

In the spring, a little over a year since it had happened, I told my sister about the sexual assault. She was working with a student organization at the university called *PAVE*: Promoting Awareness, Victim Empowerment[74]. It was an organization that would host talks at fraternities and sororities, and they did a great

---

[73] Posttraumatic Stress Disorder (PTSD) occurs in some individuals exposed to a severe life-threatening trauma. Individuals experience detachment and loss of emotional responses. Patients may feel depersonalized and unable to recall specific events of the trauma, although some may experience intrusions in thoughts, dreams, or flashbacks.

[74] PAVE is a multi-chapter national 501 c3 nonprofit organization that empowers students, parents, and civic leaders to end sexual violence with prevention education promoting respect for oneself and each other. Additionally, PAVE creates a safe space for survivors to thrive after trauma.

job educating college students – and in turn educating me. It sparked in me a realization of what had actually happened. So I shared my story with my sister. I remember exactly where we were. It was a sunny day, and I felt that it was really good, that now my sister knows, and she validated that I was indeed assaulted.

Now, I didn't feel that it was an urgent thing I needed to work through, but there were a lot of things going on with me. And I was still just a kid. I was still on my parent's health insurance, and their insurance wasn't covered in Madison, so if I wanted to see a therapist I had to figure it out for myself. I remember I was dating a guy who kind of wanted to be a therapist, and a few months into our relationship I shared my story with him. I don't remember how it happened, but I somehow realized that I wasn't living the life I wanted to be living. I realized that there were things I needed to work through. I wish I could remember how it happened that I finally did something about my life, but this isn't a beautiful story like that.

My first therapist wasn't connected to the university. I found her online, and her website said that she worked with people who had experienced sexual assault, and that she worked with college students. That helped me, because there's a stigma to seeing a therapist. Here I am coming in to talk about my stupid problems. It's not like I'm going through a divorce. I'm not coping with the death of a child. But reading her online profile helped me realize that it's okay to see a therapist about an experience like mine. And then it was a very slow unraveling – of everything. I don't think I even talked about the assault at first, but it was certainly the first thing she grabbed onto. She diagnosed me with PTSD right away. It scared the crap out of me. I thought of PTSD as a disorder of soldiers coming back from war. Getting that diagnosis really helped to validate my experience. She also recognized my anxiety and taught me tools like breathing exercises to better deal with it.

She helped me realize that I have an entirely separate identity from my family. It seems weird now, but I think a lot of people experience a phase of figuring out who they are outside of their family. I was struggling with making choices that were different from those my family made. My therapist helped me recognize why the relationship between my mother and my sister is so different from my relationship with my mother. My sister is the first-born. I remember my therapist explaining how my mom was fresh out of medical school, and she must have been terrified having a child. My mom did have anxiety, *and* depression, and my sister probably picked up on that. There is still a dynamic between them of my sister kind of protecting my mom. That is *their* relationship, and it is never going to be my relationship with my mom. Our relationship is different.

After a year of seeing her, my therapist recognized behaviors in me that she thought might be ADD[75] or ADHD. She asked to refer me to a psychiatrist. Again, I was surprised. In my mind, people with ADHD were like little trouble-maker boys in elementary class. But she taught me that ADHD is a disorder very underdiagnosed in girls and young women, and especially intelligent ones. I was the little girl in elementary raising her hand and jumping out of her seat, but it was okay, because I had the right answers.

I went to see the psychiatrist who diagnosed me with ADHD. And I tried a few medications. I ended up on a stimulant that took my depression away. It's all chemicals, just chemicals doing different things in different places of our bodies. In some people, there are more of them at the wrong time. This is how I like to

---

[75] ADD was the term used until 1987, when the word "hyperactivity" was added to the name. Attention-deficit/hyperactivity disorder (ADHD) is a brain disorder marked by an ongoing pattern of inattention and/or hyperactivity-impulsivity that interferes with functioning or development.

think about different disorders. Putting that sort of framework on it has helped me. Still, I find it crazy how just a tiny dose of a medication could clear up the fog of my depression. It was life-changing. It helped tremendously with school too. I was suddenly able to follow what my professors were saying, which wasn't something I was capable of before.

The problem was that I have anxiety, and being started on a stimulant ... well, you can imagine how that might aggravate and provoke my anxiety. So I tried an SSRI[76] for a bit, but I didn't like it. At about this time I graduated from college, moved to Seattle, and my life was becoming more stable. I realized that there were things I could do behaviorally that could really help me. I had been performing rituals as coping mechanisms for most of my life. For example, I have a bedtime routine; I have a wakeup routine. I think a lot of people probably do these things, because we are creatures of habit, but it became clear that I had incorporated these rituals into my life to help give me structure. Exercising, sleeping, eating right – everyone praises these things, yes, but for me they are absolutely

---

[76] The acute effect of a selective serotonin receptor inhibitor (SSRI) is its highly selective action on the serotonin transporter (SERT). SSRIs allosterically inhibit the transporter, binding at a site other than that of serotonin. They have minimal inhibitory effects on the norepinephrine transporter or blocking actions on adrenergic and cholinergic receptors.

essential. I have become a very particular person. There are flaws to being so particular, sure, but it is a character that has made me successful in my first year of medical school.

*Why didn't you say anything?*

It's so easy to say that. And yet here I am, and this is the first time in eight years that I have ever publicly talked about this. And I'm a feminist. I'm an outgoing, sex-positive person who is an advocate for victims of sexual assault. So what do you say to person who has experienced an assault? I think I would try to be in tune with what that person needs in the moment. It might be just to listen without judgment. Be careful what you ask them. Somebody asked me once, 'So this wouldn't have happened if you hadn't been drinking?' It was one of the most hurtful things ever said to me. Are women supposed to not drink? If you get in a car accident, you don't say to the person, *So this wouldn't have happened if you hadn't been driving?*

'What is it that you're feeling?' I would try to validate those feelings. There might be confusion. People can be raped by someone they love. You can be raped by your husband, or your wife. It's complicated.

I'm not going to sit here and say that as long as you talk about it it's easy. But you have to support them. *I believe you. I support you.* Ask what they need from you. But be careful with their boundaries. It can be damaging to push too far without permission.

There's just no one right way to heal.

I was starting my first semester of medical school when somebody close to me called. She asked if I could help a mutual friend who had been sexual assaulted. She had a difficult time asking me. She felt it was a burden, but she knew she wasn't the person our friend needed right then. So I called our mutual friend and I talked with her. We talked for hours. I had a lot to say. And, you know, it felt almost empowering. For the first time I realized how far I had come. I realized that I could help people. From the lessons of my struggle, maybe I could help prevent someone from falling into the same cycle of silence that I had fallen into.

# JUSTIN

*I've taken the mindset that my symptoms are a self-cognitive behavioral response of trying to understand the things that happened to me. I can change how I think about it, but I can't change 'it'.*

## *Post Traumatic Stress Disorder*

IT BEGAN IN 2012, my first year in the military. This was about six years ago now, and I still experience symptoms – but it was during finals of last semester, my first semester of medical school, when the insomnia started. I didn't know what it was about, and I'm still trying to understand it. I used to have nightmares after the incident. It's a part of PTSD.

I grew up in Florida and I had a pretty good childhood for the most part. My dad says that I had issues growing up, issues with different day cares and schools, things like that. I think it was mostly related to my mother leaving. She left me with my father. And growing up without a mom, her leaving me when I was just a kid, it was *big*. I know that traumatic events can be triggers for mental health conditions, but I wouldn't attribute the symptoms I experience today to that experience.

After high school, I spent one year at a community college – but I wanted to get out of the small town I was in. I've always had an urge to serve my country, so I joined the military. The United States Army. I was an infantryman for four years. I feel no resentment looking back. Those four years were an amazing experience and they really made me into the person I am today. I'm very proud and honored to have served my country.

Now I imagine everyone is probably assuming that this is a combat-related story … but it's not.

Throughout much of my service, I was deployed in countries like Thailand and Korea; we stayed in the Pacific too. We didn't go to Iraq or Afghanistan. My time was non-combatant. I was stationed in Hawaii. And I would hang out with the guys who liked to party. We were young. I was living it up, going downtown, and I just didn't consider situations like what ended up happening.

We went out one night and had dinner, a few drinks. My buddy and I were heading back to base. It happened so quickly. There was a gang. They were hanging out in downtown. When they saw us, they misidentified my friend, and thought he was part of a past fight. Of course, he wasn't related to any kind of gang or anything like that. It was just the wrong place, the wrong time.

I remember we were walking back to our car. Out of nowhere my friend says to me, 'Hey get ready, these guys are coming at us.' He had grown up in rough neighborhoods. He could see what was about to go down. There were nine of them. They ran up on us and one of them knocked my friend out – one hit – and then a group of them were surrounding and kicking him, and the next thing I know I was grappling with a guy. I didn't understand it at first. I was looking into this guy's face. He was right in front of me. Then someone came up behind me, grabbed my shoulder …

A knife slide into my side, slowly.

It pulled out, jabbed in again.

And again.

I didn't know what to do. I knew I had to stay alive; I had to keep this knife from going any further, or into a spot that would have killed me. I was still wrestling with the guy in front of me and I threw him at the person who was stabbing me. And I backed up, just swinging. I knew that if I went down these guys would kill me. I was saying to myself – *Just stay alive. Keep these guys away from your friend. They're going to kill him.* I kept backing away, swinging, trying to get out of it, when out of nowhere one of them starts yelling, 'Let's go! Let's go!' And they ran off. They just ran off.

I remember looking at my friend. He was out cold. His face was bloody. I tried to get him up, but he wouldn't wake. I was saying – 'Get up, come on, get up.' It took a long time, and he finally came around. We were walking away and my side was killing me. My whole side, all of my abdomen, it was drenched. I was bleeding out. And I was starting to have trouble breathing. I remember holding onto my side, taking these short breaths. In that moment my lung collapsed. I was trying to get to this pole in the main strip. I could barely walk, but I wanted to get to that pole. And when I reached it, finally, I sat down. I don't think my friend realized what had happened. He had been unconscious.

He ran off and flagged down a police officer, and when the officer came he saw right away that I was in a critical condition.

I began going in and out of consciousness.

I remember a person walking down the strip who came up to me. I was saying to him – 'I don't want to die, I don't want to die' – and he was telling me, 'I got you, man. You're not going to die.' He was talking to me trying to keep me awake. But I was fading in and out. There was so much pain.

It was an out-of-body experience.

I remember the ambulance pulling up. Everything gets foggy. They start injecting me with fluids. A moment passes like a blur and I'm being carted into an ER. They take me to a room, rip off all of my clothes. I'm lying naked under a fluorescent light. *Is this it? Am I going to die?* I was too young. I was only nineteen or twenty years old. I was scared. *This can't be it. I don't want to die.*

You're faced with the fact that you have to be willing to die when you're in the military. If you go to war. Automatically I think, *Yes, that's okay. That's what I want to do. I want to serve my country. I don't want to die, but I'm willing to risk my life for my country.* This is something that every military man has to come to terms with.

But when it hit me that I might actually die in this moment – *I might die right here under this fluorescent light* – I wasn't prepared for it. My family wasn't with me. I was alone. Everything was happening so fast. I was naked on a table in front of about eight people in a hospital in Honolulu when the doctor walked in. And I remember thinking in that moment: *Everything's going to be okay now. This guy has got me. He's got me. He's going to do everything and I'm going to be okay.*

They did an MRI to see if any of my abdominal structures were damaged. I can remember the anesthesiologist coming into the room and saying to me – 'We're going to have to put you under now; you're going to the O.R.' Then I floated off.

I woke up five or six hours later. There was a chest tube sticking out of me. I remember feeling a little out of it because of the drugs. Then my friend walked into the room, my friend who was with me during the incident. He had bruises and a couple scratches on his face. And I was so glad because it had looked like he was taking a worse beating than me. 'Man, I'm so sorry,' he said to me. We just looked at each other. Both of us were so relieved. We had made it through the night.

I was really lucky. The surgeons had searched all through my stomach for any damage, and one of the punctures was very close to my liver, but it must have bisected through a channel that didn't have any arteries or major nerves. I was really lucky. But my lung was collapsed, and each day we were waiting for it to open back up. I still have symptoms sometimes, like wheezing in my lower lobe.

I was drugged up most of the time, so I don't remember all that much of it actually, but I was in the hospital for about three weeks. Florida's a long way from Hawaii, so I didn't have any family with me. But I wanted to get back to my military unit. I wanted to feel safe again. Those were the guys I spent my days with. They came to visit when they could, but they were busy. So, yes, I wanted to get out of the hospital. And I've been a runner my whole life. I ran cross-country. I ran in the army. I was a ten-mile runner in the army, so I didn't want to lose that part of me – being one of the top soldiers in my battalion – I didn't want to lose my health.

I started running again six or seven months later. I took it slow each day. Coming back from recovery, I made small steps, small goals. I still have problems with my right lower lobe; it still hurts to take deep breaths. I don't think my lung will ever be one-hundred percent again, but I'm pretty well off.

After the hospital, I went on leave to recuperate. I stayed in my barracks room and didn't go out much. The guys went off on missions, so I was by myself a lot of the time. I think this is when the symptoms first started to manifest, but I didn't notice them because I wasn't going out. I wasn't talking to people. I wasn't thinking about it. After about six months, when the guys started coming back and I started hanging out with people again, going out for dinner and drinks, I found myself keeping my back to the wall in crowds. I became hyper-vigilant, very aware of my surroundings. You're trained in the military to be aware of your surroundings, but I found myself paying *much* more attention to my environment. I would watch people around me. I would try to interpret what they were doing. Are they here for dinner? Are they here to be with family? I was wary of large groups. I would look for gang tattoos. It became stressful for me to be in crowded places.

I didn't understand PTSD. I waived off the symptoms. Being in the military, there's an underlying macho factor that you have to be all the man you can be. You have to do this for the person next to you. You can't think, *What's going on with me emotionally? What am I feeling right now?* You're taught to think about how you're going to help the soldier next to you in a combat situation. And you don't want to show signs of weakness. You don't want people to think they can't count on you. So I tried really hard to shake off the feelings. *I'm okay. It'll go away. I have to be strong for everyone.* It was only much later that I learned that this is not even close to healthy behavior.

I began having a recurrent nightmare. Instead of being stabbed, I'd be shot. I'd be lying by that pole in downtown Honolulu and bleeding. I remember waking up from that dream a lot. I probably had that dream every two or three weeks. Now I've always had issues with sleep. I've never taken medication for anxiety, but

I did take *Ambien*[77] for sleep. Still, you kind of learn how to function off of four or five hours sleep in the military, so I never attributed my not sleeping to PTSD – more just to my occupation. I'm in the military. I do what I have to do. And I have to wake up at 5am, or 4am, or whatever the call may be. But those nightmares hit me hard.

About nine months after the incident, we went into the field for two months for training and running missions. When I was out there, for whatever reason, my mind would clear up. I could focus on what I was doing in the moment. You have to do your job when you're on mission. But then we would come back and I would start having thoughts of these first-responder type scenarios. *What would I do if an active shooter was here right now? What if somebody was stabbed right here in front of me? What would I do then?* I still have these thoughts. I was experiencing symptoms too, like the avoidance I mentioned before, and the nightmares. Everything else I could attribute to part of the military experience, but I just didn't understand PTSD.

---

[77] Ambien (Trade), Zolpidem (generic). Zolpidem is used to treat a certain sleep problem (insomnia) in adults. If you have trouble falling asleep, it helps you fall asleep faster, so you can get a better night's rest. Zolpidem belongs to a class of drugs called sedative-hypnotics. It acts on your brain to produce a calming effect. This medication is usually limited to short treatment periods of 1 to 2 weeks or less.

I went to my platoon leader and I told him, 'Look, I'm having all these thoughts, not suicidal thoughts, not depression –and I'm having these nightmares –and I'm feeling hyper-vigilance in crowds. I need to do something.'

They sent me to a therapist. But in the military, it's hard to keep a schedule with a therapist; at least in the infantry, you're constantly leaving for the field, going on missions, so it's hard to keep any schedule at all. I really only opened up to the therapist about the superficial story of what had happened to me. Not much came of it. And, you know, I just didn't connect with her like I might have if I had had more time and sessions. But she did identify the symptoms I was experiencing as those of PTSD. I remember the shock I felt. *Wow. I didn't even go to combat. There's no way I can be experiencing PTSD. I have squad leaders who have been shot in the face. I've known soldiers with their legs blown off. That's PTSD.*

But you can't compare one man's tragedy to another.

I went back and revisited that pole I was lying against when I was bleeding and scared that night. It was a long time after. I remember feeling lightheaded, dissociated, unable to stay in the moment. It felt surreal and out-of-body. I couldn't think. But I think that by being there it helped me to understand what happened. It brought back a lot of memories.

*I made it through that night. I survived.*

It's funny, because my wife now, I met her in downtown Honolulu. She lived a block away from that pole, and the first time I met her we were at a pool that was overlooking the back alley where I was stabbed. I remember thinking how it was right down there where I almost died. Just over there. Across the road. I didn't tell her that though.

When I was in the military, I didn't do anything to manage my PTSD. I just kept playing the macho card. It wasn't until I started undergrad again that it really hit me. I was out of the military by then. I was more alone. I didn't know anybody at the college I was at. And I was married now. I remember thinking that I needed to do something about my PTSD. The nightmares were recurring every week, and I was becoming more and more anxious in crowds. I would often be preoccupied in class with thoughts of what I would do if someone suddenly came in with a knife. What would I do? What can I do? It was getting out of control.

My wife has a background in psychology, and so I think that hearing about cognitive behavioral therapy from her in passing, and even coming upon it when I was studying for the MCAT, has been really beneficial for me. It's a great way to think about what's happening, because if you can approach it from this different perspective, you can stop it from growing into a monster. I think I did everything right too. I was exercising. I was taking care of myself emotionally. I found a good group of study-buddies. Over time I began to realize that when I was out and about in crowds, I was okay. *Nobody's going to do anything to you. It's going to be okay. No one's going to come up behind you. No one's going to stab you.* I've learned to talk myself through anxiety when I feel it coming on, because I still experience it sometimes. I might feel that somebody is following me, and I'll ask myself, why would this person be following me? They're probably just going home. Everything is okay.

If anyone has gone through a trauma and is experiencing elements of PTSD, I would tell them that although each individual is different, seek help. Seek help immediately. Look for a therapist. Talk to people who have had similar experiences. Try to understand why you're feeling these things. Try to understand why you're experiencing these symptoms. Once you talk to somebody, and once you start to understand it, it becomes less of a monster; and, more importantly, you learn how to stop feeding that monster.

I met my wife[78] while I was in the military. She was planning to go to medical school, and so I thought to myself – *Well, I've got to do something* – and so we applied together, and we were both accepted. We're one of only two married couples in our class.

I've learned to accept that what happened to me – yes, it's fucked up and, no, I can't change it – but the thoughts that I'm having now, I can change those. I've taken the mindset that my symptoms are a self-cognitive behavioral response of trying to understand the things that happened to me. I can change how I think about it, but I can't change *it*. This has really

---

[78] 'Stacy, if you're there, I love you.'

helped me. The nightmares are gone now; they just kind of faded away.

# RICHARD

*I am one of the many unwilling to seek help.*

***Undiagnosed
Child of Paranoid Schizophrenic***

I HAVE A FAMILY HISTORY of paranoid schizophrenia[79] [80], bipolar depression, anger, anxiety, abandonment, and I'm not sure if I have a behavioral health disorder. I am one of the many unwilling to seek help. My father was also unwilling to seek help. I watched his life deteriorate because of his refusal to acknowledge mental illness; he lost everything except for his money. The damage he caused to those closest to him was devastating.

---

[79] Paranoid Type Schizophrenia, as per the Diagnostic and Statistical Manual of Mental Disorders, 4th Edition (DSM IV), was diagnosed when the following criteria were met: 1. preoccupation with one or more delusions or frequent auditory hallucinations; 2. none of the following was prominent: disorganized speech, disorganized or catatonic behavior, or flat or inappropriate affect.

[80] It is important to note that the 5th edition of the DSM has now dropped Paranoid Type, along with dropping disorganized, catatonic, undifferentiated, and residual subtype. The rationale for doing away with these subtypes is they are not stable conditions, and have not afforded significant clinical utility, nor scientific validity and reliability.

Yet here I am, a first-year medical student with a primary interest in psychiatry – I can't help but acknowledge the irony that I am unwilling to assess my own emotional health. Is it pride keeping me from speaking aloud self-doubt? Is it fear that a diagnosis would seal my fate to that of my father? Perhaps, alternatively, I'm just fine. Maybe I'm no different than anybody else. We all feel a little *crazy* sometimes, right? I probably don't need help anyway. I have friends, meaningful relationships, a loving family. I actively pursue my dreams. I have purpose in my life. I'm fine.

My father probably reassured himself with these very testaments.

But I fear that I am losing pieces of myself gradually. I don't relate to others like I once did. This was the great gift of my character. And I anger so easily now, particularly toward those whom I love; people spark in me such distain. I push them away for no reason. I feel myself filling with resentment. I feel overcome by insecurity. Are these flaws in my character? Is medical school simply digging its nails into my psyche? Or are these manifestations of an undiagnosed and progressing mental illness?

\*   \*   \*

I was raised in the southernmost tip of Texas, on the border by the sea, and so naturally I wanted to be a fisherman when I grew up. I wanted to drift the Gulf of Mexico, float under the stars, and share my life with somebody who would love me unconditionally. When my grandpa took me deep-sea fishing, I vomited for four straight hours. It was terrible. I realized that I might not be cut out for a fisherman's life. But I think my dream was for adventure and romance and not necessarily working as a fisherman. I wanted to be like my Grandpa. He had traveled the world, raised a family, maintained a life-long marriage, and he was a doctor. And yet, I don't know why, or where this belief originated, I understood from a very early age that I just wasn't smart enough to become a doctor.

My father was a lawyer; my mother was a secretary for a state congressman – and so my sister and I were half-raised by a nanny named *Lichita* from Guanajuato. She was the loveliest woman. She never had children of her own and loved my sister and I as though we were hers. Lichita lived with us through my formative youth and then disappeared back into Mexico. I didn't see her again for many years.

I remember the first time my father slapped me. It was a distinct transition in my childhood. I must have been six or seven, and my sister and I were fighting over something trivial. I stomped on her foot because she had an ingrown toenail and I wanted whatever we were fighting over. She started crying, and my father rushed over, held me up against the wall and slapped me. He slapped me hard across my face. I remember the shock. I realized an element of danger in my father in that moment, and I ran off crying, not for the physical pain of having been hit, but for the sense of loss from my protector. My father, however, was not a particularly abusive man, not physically – he was emotionally abusive. He would affirm his dominance over us in curious ways. He tossed my shoes in the *resaca*[81] because I left them in the middle of the living room; in his way, he was trying to teach me something. He cut the telephone cord to my bedroom to let me know of his dissatisfaction that I was on the phone too much. I woke up one day to find the wooden dining room table had been thrown through the sliding glass door into the swimming pool. I still don't know why he

---

[81] A dry channel or marshy course of a stream; a former channel from which the Rio Grande River once flowed before it changed its course.

did that. He pulled me aside one day and told me that he was going to send me to boarding school because I was too difficult a child. I was seven years old. I remember being terribly frightened, and I remember the relief when my mother said she would *never* send me away. These events seem trivial now, decades later, but there was a tension in our household that I can distinctly recall.

My father suffered terrible anger. He was also a bipolar depressive. He inherited this from his own father, my other grandfather, whom I have very fond memories of. I knew him as a solitary and somewhat grumpy old man, but always kind. My father's relationship with him was much more volatile. On holidays, my mother would drive my sister and I to San Antonio to stay with her family. My father never joined us. He would predictably suffer a depressive spell in the week to two weeks before any family holiday, and he would isolate himself in his and my mother's bedroom. I would hear the television playing and see light from the slit under the door that was always locked. I used to press my face to the floor and peer in and look for his shadow moving across the carpet. He would come out now and again like a zombie, shuffle to the kitchen, then shuffle back to his room and lock the door again.

My mother tells me how logical and reasonable he could be. She had recorded a chart depicting the cyclicality of his bipolar episodes over a number of years and showed it to him. She tells me he was surprised by it, that he had not recognized the cyclical nature of his episodes, nor had he correlated them to holidays or family events. My mother tells me how fun he could be.

I only have fleeting memories of my father –

I see him swimming in the pool. He uses free weights to keep count of his laps. I'm playing in the shallow end and he swims over to me and lifts me out of the water. I'm looking into his round face. His eyes are the lightest blue and there's a gap between his front teeth and he's smiling up at me. Then he throws me.

I hear the front door brushing the Saltillo tiles as my father arrives home from work. I'm curled on the sofa in the living room, the television is playing, and I bury myself a little deeper into the cushions. I don't make a sound. I can hear him walking through the kitchen, and his footsteps nearing the sofa. He reaches down suddenly, and I flinch; he's tickling me. I'm squealing and kicking and he's tickling me.

First, he moved out of the house and into the pool room in the garage. Ultimately, he left the home altogether and slowly faded from our lives. I was nine years old. He refused to pay child support. He began transferring his finances out of the country, convinced that my mother and the government were trying to abscond him of his wealth. He believed that what he earned in his legal career over the decades of his marriage belonged exclusively to him –and not to his family –and certainly not to his wife. My father was always intelligent, but paranoia[82] seemed to overtake his logic. He was a man who thrived in adversity. It is likely this quality that made him so formidable a trial attorney. He was articulate, obsessive in detail, and unrelenting in a fight. And now, I don't know why, but he aimed his fight against his family.

And so began my father's personal and professional ruin. In the three-year-long court battle of divorce proceedings, I believe his paranoia evolved into schizophrenia[83]. He became convinced that my mother

---

[82] Paranoia involves intense anxious or fearful feelings and thoughts often related to persecution, threat, or conspiracy. Paranoia can become delusions, when irrational thoughts and beliefs become so fixed that nothing, including contrary evidence, can convince a person that what they think or feel is not true.

[83] Schizophrenia is a chronic and severe mental disorder that affects how a person thinks, feels, and behaves. These individuals may seem like

was indoctrinating my sister and I against him. He became seized by a delusion that his wife and children were attempting to rob him and destroy him. I think he likely suffered a mental breakdown. But he suffered it alone. Was it pride keeping him from speaking aloud any self-doubt? Maybe he was afraid that a diagnosis would seal his fate to that of his own father. I was nine, and then ten, and then eleven, and I didn't understand what was happening. I only knew that my father was gone and my mother was struggling. My mother was learning how to become a single mom, how to financially support herself and her children, and how to confront life without her partner. She had been a somewhat submissive wife for twenty-five years. And so began my mother's personal and professional rebirth.

When it was uncovered in court that my father had transferred the bulk of the marital finances out of the country, which he did meticulously and with very little paper footprint, and that he was acting in his own best interests and not those of his children, and certainly not toward any equitable divide between spouses, the court awarded my mother the various commercial real estate that my parents had invested in throughout the years of their marriage. The problem was that there

---

they have lost touch with reality. It can be extremely disabling. These individuals may have hallucinations, delusions, agitated body movements, and reduced expression of emotions.

were outstanding debts remaining on all the properties, the majority of the tenants had vacated, an arsonist had set fire to the most lucrative building, and all liquid monies had been depleted from the joint accounts. I didn't know any this at the time. I was only a child. My mother tried to keep my sister and I reasonably informed, but she must have struggled in finding an appropriate balance. How much do you tell a child of the implications of parental abandonment?

We started seeing a therapist. We went as a family, the three of us, and then I began seeing her privately. Her name was Jane. She was older, very kind; I would sit in a big chair and we would talk. She would ask me how I was feeling. She would ask me about school. I had just left elementary school and transitioned into the sixth grade in a middle school where I didn't know anybody. All my friends were zoned to a different middle school. I remember my grandfather passed away that year, my father's dad. It was at his funeral that I saw my father for the last time. I remember not knowing how to act around him –if I should hug him –if I should go to dinner with him. I hadn't seen him in a while, and I was aware that my father wasn't an active part of my life any longer. I talked about it with Jane. We talked about a lot of things.

I suppose therapy was beneficial. It was certainly necessary for my mother. Her death and rebirth was profound, and she needed someone to help guide her through it. But for me, the transition was actually quite fluid. I never felt particularly lacking for a father. I had always identified with my mother. From a rather young age, I felt something of a protective instinct toward her, whereas toward my father I can only recall ever feeling apprehension. I would ask my mother about him from time to time –

"What was he like when you two were in love?"
*He was fun. He was the life of the party.*

"Why did he leave?"
*I don't know, honey, but it's not your fault.*

"Will I ever see him again?"
*I think you will. Someday.*

---

[84] Paranoid personality disorder (PPD) is a mental condition in which a person has a long-term pattern of distrust and suspicion of others. The person does not have a full-blown psychotic disorder, such as schizophrenia. PPD seems to be more common in men.

My mother had maintained a dysfunctional marriage for twenty-five years to an unchecked bipolar depressive with paranoid personality disorder[84], fickle resentment, and explosive anger. After the divorce, she made a promise to my sister and I that she would not date another man until we were grown and moved away. She wanted us to know that her love was exclusively for us. She became a business woman, became active in local politics, won a seat as city commissioner. She always emphasized the benefits of travel and culture, and she showed us the world. My mother filled the void in my life of an absent father. She would take me fishing, and camping; she taught me how to handle weapons, and how to cook, and how to bookkeep. She introduced men from our community into my life that I might emulate. Mr. Lucio was a bail bondsman, strong, brash, perhaps a bit *machismo*[85], which is to say exceptionally masculine, but a man of great warmth; he took me horseback riding for years. Judge Vela was a federal circuit judge, calm, sincere, thoughtful and respected; he believed in me academically, taught me to balance right and wrong and to always pursue the good. Then there was my Grandpa, my mother's dad, the patriarch of my extended family – the doctor. He was kind, intelligent, compassionate and adventurous; orphaned in his

---

[85] Machismo is defined as a strong sense of pride or exaggerated masculinity.

childhood, he valued family above all things. I consciously try to shape my character off of these men, and off of my mother, and even off of the bits and pieces of my father that I think were positive.

Although absent for the majority of my life, my father has certainly influenced me in ways beyond the genetic inheritances that might or might not prove my detriment. He was an individual capable of great triumphs when he was able to overcome the weight of his emotions. I used to wonder if he was looking in on my life. I thought I saw him more than a few times over the years, peeking in on me like I used to peek under the slit of his locked door, just hoping to catch a glimpse. What would we have said to one another? I liked to imagine us in a bar, sitting side by side, and I would *not* ask him all the questions he was probably afraid of being asked. I would just listen to the story of his life and tell him the story of mine. I think I made a lot of life decisions in anticipation of such a moment.

I went to a magnet school called Med-High. It was my introduction to practical medicine. I was always more of an extracurricular student than an academic student, and I think this has benefitted me tremendously over the years because I enjoyed school. I still enjoy school – well, first-year medical school is actually quite distressing, but I actively balance the academics by participating in extracurriculars. My mother always spoke of education with the implicit understanding that I would go to college and then to graduate school, and so I always believed higher education to be the natural progression. I never questioned it. I was only an okay student, certainly not exceptional. Although I would have loved to pursue a path toward medicine, I sincerely believed that such a path was reserved exclusively for the most exceptional students. Medicine was simply beyond me. I moved to Colorado for college. I wanted adventure. I studied English and had the romantic idea of traveling the world as a writer like Hemingway. I would have preferred to travel the world with a medical kit as a doctor, but I knew that the pre-medical sciences were beyond me. I never tested this theory. I only believed it. I wasn't smart enough for medicine.

Insecurity in its various forms has been perhaps the more crippling curse in my life. I don't know where it stems from, but it can be debilitating. I have never felt intelligent or perceived myself as intelligent. I often assume that people are confused by my academic successes when they meet me and realize that I'm actually not all that smart. My protective instinct is to become quiet, so that I don't expose my lack of intuition. I wonder where in childhood such self-doubt originates, for it was certainly at a very young age that I accepted my intellectual mediocrity, and yet I recognized that my parents and sister were each highly intelligent.

It was at about this time in my life, when I was graduating from high-school and preparing to move to Colorado for college, that my mother found Lichita living in a shack across the border in Matamoros. Lichita, who had nurtured me through my childhood and loved me in my youth. She was blind now from cataracts[86]. Her leg had been amputated as a result of gangrenous diabetes[87]. Her nephew had robbed her of her life savings. I suppose I was at an influential age, but I recognized the disparity of our lives, and the impact that health education and medical access can have on a person. My mother arranged for cataract surgery, and Lichita cried when she finally saw us again. She moved to a church-sponsored home and spent her days in a wheelchair under the sun with the other old folks who had no families.

---

[86] A cataract is a clouding of the normally clear lens of your eye. Clouded vision can make it more difficult to reach and drive a car. Most cataracts develop slowly, and are most effectively treated with surgery.

[87] Diabetes is a disease in which your blood glucose levels are too high. Over time, having too much glucose in your blood can damage your eyes, kidneys, and nerves. Eventually, diabetes can also cause heart disease, stroke and the need to remove a limb.

I worked as a nursing assistant toward the end of college. There are so many elderly residents who face their final years alone. For a great many, the nursing staff become a kind of surrogate family. It was the most fulfilling job I ever had. Then I moved back to Texas and began studying law. The transition from English to Law is not uncommon, and although I never wanted to be a lawyer like my father, I knew I wasn't smart enough to become a doctor like my grandpa. I hadn't taken any of the prerequisite sciences necessary to even apply to medical school. But law school was a wonderful experience and education, and it was absolutely essential to my ultimate pursuit of medicine. I learned two of the greatest lessons of my life in law school: (i) how to study; and (ii) that I am capable of handling higher academics. I promised myself that if I didn't discover a passion for the law, then I would return to undergrad, complete the premedical coursework and make the push for medicine.

I graduated from law school and immediately enrolled at a community college to begin studying the foundational sciences. It took me a year and a half, during which time I longed for the great adventures I had been postponing all my life in pursuit of education. You see, being a committed student demands tremendous emotional energy. All through my undergraduate studies, and law school, and the year-and-a-half of pre-medical sciences, I would often take a step back and consciously assess my emotional health. Am I a bipolar depressive like my father? I think yes. Am I destined to be alone because of it? I think probably. Is it fair to get married and have children and expose them to my genetics? I think not. I foresaw a solitary existence, and I was okay with that. Then, instead of applying to medical school, I decided that it was time to start living a very different dream.

All of my life I had been a student. Now I wanted to test myself in the world. I drove to Minnesota, moved in with a college friend, and worked nights in the warehouse of a huge beer distributor. I met a girl who sold flowers at a farmer's market and fell in love. I spent two years in Minnesota, then I sold my car and bought a one-way ticket to Southeast Asia. I didn't know anybody. I wandered through Laos and Cambodia and when I ran out of money I settled in the northern jungles of Thailand. I rented a motorbike and knocked on the doors of various English departments at universities and foreign language schools. I became an English teacher at Chiang Mai University. I lived in that jungle paradise for two years and I almost stayed there indefinitely. but I moved back to Texas to spend time with my grandparents. They were in their nineties and it was important to me to be involved in their lives. I became a wedding photographer at my mother's wedding venue. These next years, although I loved being with my family, I felt stagnant. I struggled emotionally. In one hand I balanced the guilt of wanting to leave, and in the other I suppressed a longing to embark upon a new adventure, to set out for somewhere completely unknown and filled with possibility.

I find that I am happiest in the exhilaration of the unknown. I move and create a life for myself, a wonderful life of friends, a loving partner, happiness and satisfaction – and then the same dark cloud inevitably drifts nearer. It creeps over my life slowly. I become bored, frustrated by people; what was exciting before turns routine. And so I pack up my life and move away. I think it is my form of therapy. The intense sadness I feel in leaving is overcome by a great rush of endorphins[88] in anticipation of what is to come. And I don't mind the sadness. I learned as a nursing assistant that sorrow is counterbalanced by joy – the death of someone I have loved is worth the joy I experienced by

---

[88] Endorphins interact with receptors in your brain that reduce your perception of pain, similar to that of morphine. Endorphins are released when you exercise, and are manufactured in your brain, spinal cord, and other parts of your body. The activation of endorphin receptors does not lead to addiction or dependence.

their life. So it was with Grandma, and Grandpa, and Mr. Lucio, and Judge Vela, and my flower-girl in Minnesota who I shared two years of my life with. Sadness is a big part of my life, perhaps because I am a bipolar depressive, or perhaps because it is a part of everybody's life. I have learned to embrace sadness.

My life was stagnant in Texas. It was during a weekend trip when I was driving my Grandpa back from his seventy-fifth medical school reunion at Baylor when I decided that I would pursue medicine again. It had been seven years since I had completed the premedical coursework, and I knew it would be a two-year process to gain a seat at a medical school. It was a gamble. I might not be accepted at all. But I packed my car for one last adventure, and I drove to Alaska. There would be no distractions in Alaska. I could study for the MCAT[89] through the darkness of winter and shadow physicians through the brightness of summer. I left my life behind one more time. I think I needed to be alone. I have always had elements of deep solitude within me. I wonder if this isn't a remnant of my father; he too was a solitary man.

---

[89] The Medical College Admission Test (MCAT) has been part of the medical school admission process for more than 90 years. Each year, more than 85,000 students sit for the exam. Nearly all medical schools in the United States and some in Canada require the MCAT. The exam is 7 hours and 30 minutes long and is taken over the course of one day.

My father left Texas after the divorce; in fact, he left the United States altogether and moved to Vancouver, Canada, or so I heard. His mother, my grandmother, lived in Portland, Oregon, and I suppose he wanted to be close to her. It is a characteristic that we shared, a fondness for our mothers. I heard later that he moved to Mexico City. I often wondered of my father. I liked to imagine that he was happy and in love, with a new family and children, somewhere in the world, reflecting now and again upon his life long ago in Texas. I found him in Costa Rica the year before I moved to Alaska. He was in a coma. I flew to San Jose and navigated the convoluted public hospital system, and finally there he was, unconscious and intubated. His chest rose and fell dramatically with the force of the automatic respirator that was keeping him alive. He looked how I remembered, and it was surreal to see my features in him. I saw my nose, and the structure of my face, and the fineness of my hair. Twenty-five years ago, he lifted me out of the swimming pool and held me up high and I looked upon this very face.

He died six months later. I returned to Costa Rica, went to the morgue and identified my father, and I helped carry his body into a kind of hearse. I arranged for his cremation and brought his remains back to

Texas. It was the conclusion to a significant part of my life.

I think my father lost many of the joys of his life to unacknowledged mental health disorders. He simply could not balance his emotions or reason against the weight of his mental anguish, although he tried, and he likely believed that he was managing quite well. Perhaps this is enough then to say that he was. Objectively, however, his disorder led him to the mistaken belief that his wife and children were rivals, that his wife had brain-washed his children against him, and that he had to safeguard his material wealth from the government and his family. He was unwilling or unable to acknowledge his part in the dissolution of both his business and his family. What a terrible tragedy – that my father, a man of absolute potential, in the relative start of raising a family, lost everything to his unchecked mental health.

I'm studying for finals now. The end of first-year medical school is only a few weeks away. I have to keep my feelings in check. I might become unreasonably angry. I might feel trivialized by a colleague or professor. I feel horribly alone, unloved, unwanted, burdensome. I am immersed in a pool of the most intelligent students and faculty imaginable. I wonder why they haven't realized that I don't belong here amongst them. It is so easy to be consumed by my emotions. I have to remind myself that these feelings are a normal response to the stresses of what seems at times the most overwhelming endeavor.

*Do I need help?*

I don't know. But I'm not doing this alone. I fell in love in Alaska with a third-year medical student. She showed me the way of medicine and medical school. We went ice fishing on Chena Lake in late December as the northern lights were twisting and weaving across the sky and we didn't catch a thing, but we fell in love. I dreamt of fishing beside her when I was only a child. Yes, I am imbalanced, without a doubt, but I am also very lucky. I have to remind myself of this. It is easy to forget.

*Finding the Balance*

# MEDICAL SCHOOL
## FIRST YEAR FINALLY WRAPPING UP

The tsunami sweeps over everything in your life, draws you into that dark and lonely place. You've been here before. The pressure is overwhelming. But you mustn't stop struggling. You must paddle with all the more ferocity and remind yourself that you wanted this. It is a privilege to be studying medicine. You are here because you have proven that you have the characteristics of a medical student, and the potential to help.

*Maturity. Empathy. Tenacity. Grit.*

To be diagnosed with a behavioral health disorder is no longer a deterrent to reaching the dream of medicine. It might even be the case that there are more of us with behavioral health disorders than without. Yet so many of us are silent. So many of us are unwilling to acknowledge having such a disorder – for so long as there remains a stigma associated with being different, and especially of the mind, there will remain some measure of shame and some measure of concealment. This has been the history of behavioral health.

Something remarkable happened in the first semester of first year. Behavioral health came to the forefront of discussion outside of the classroom. And there was no shame associated with it. There was no judgement toward those who acknowledged diagnoses. Every student seemed to relate in some way, either by living with such a disorder or knowing somebody diagnosed.

It began with Logan Noone.

I met him walking into orientation. He was bright-eyed and excited. We spoke of our mutual astonishment that we had been accepted into medical school, for we both undervalued our capabilities. Then Logan surprised me. He told me that he lived with bipolar depression. He said it so casually. I remember being slightly taken aback. I had never met an individual so open to a behavioral health diagnosis before. You can see Logan's strength of character, how he exposes his vulnerabilities so readily. And as is often the case with a person who shares something so intimate, which is a kind of invitation to lay down your guard, I reciprocated and told Logan of my own family history with behavioral health. I told him of the wreckage my father's untreated bipolar depression had upon my family. And then I reevaluated what it meant to be an individual with a behavioral health disorder.

*It is a disorder only in so much as it disrupts your life.*

Logan asks me if I would speak of my emotional struggles. He emphasizes the therapeutic value of communication in the management of his own behavioral health. My reflex is silence, letting others talk about themselves when I know I should be expressing my own fears and anxieties. I am accustomed to resolving my difficulties in private, hidden away from whatever shame or judgment might be waiting – and yet aware that such fears are fictitious. Is it pride thus keeping me from acknowledging a weakness?

I reflect upon my colleagues. Megan lifted herself from despair with the help of her family and friends. Neelou could have easily given in to her anxiety but instead returned and tackled first year for a second time. Augustus showed me that you can consciously channel your focus. Daniella is an example that it is possible to raise a child and balance a family while tackling both medical school and emotional health. I think of Laura and how she chases her dreams to the end. I think of Ted climbing Mount Denali, which he will do in a few months to recharge after first year finally wraps up. It is his therapy. Heather walks the halls of our medical school and you can see how strong she is in how she carries herself. Justin overcame his nightmares with the help of his wife who is also his colleague; they are a power team in our school, and they will be in medicine as well. These students have each embraced communication as an initial step in the management of hers and his behavioral health.

Although my instinct is to guard myself in silence, I sit down with Logan and tell him of my life. I'm not sure if my emotions are causing me irreparable detriment. Perhaps my father wondered the same – although it is clear on hindsight that his life was spiraling beyond his control. It is difficult to acknowledge such a personal and stigmatized disorder of the mind. It is easier to direct blame at others than to acknowledge that the origin of depression might just be *me*. It feels like a flaw. An imperfection in my character. Like I have failed in something that I should have had control over.

Medicine. The strain of first year is nearing its peak and I can't stop running. I can't slow down. I just hope I pass Anatomy. I hope I pass Respiratory. I might not. I am always on the edge. There will be setbacks in my life: I will be knocked down, and I will get back up, and I will be knocked down again. I think it is an unspoken part of the medical education to instill in us the resolve to get up one more time.

Just a few more weeks left.

Perhaps first year medical school is a kind of death and rebirth. It breaks us, dissects us, instructs us on the workings of the human body while prodding and poking our vulnerable minds. Then it molds us into a very specific shape. Our newly formed arms reach through the sleeves of a long white coat. Our newly molded heads extend about the loop of a stethoscope. Doctors are born into images of perfection. We are created into minds that are assumed unflawed and in perfect balance.

But medicine is inherently imperfect, and so are we. We hold ourselves to such high standards – it can be devastating. Our emotional health must be consciously nurtured. We must take ownership of it. A behavioral health disorder offers a unique perspective to the experience of life, but it need not be a detriment to your dreams. And so continue the struggle, and persist, and if you are one of us, and the time is right, come into medicine. We need people who can accomplish great things for others, and who can understand what it is like.

## Endnotes

1. Insomnia. *U.S. National Library of Medicine.* https://medlineplus.gov/insomnia.html. Accessed April 2, 2019.

2. Holy Cross at a Glance. *College of the Holy Cross.* https://www.holycross.edu/about-holy-cross/holy-cross-glance. Accessed April 2, 2019.

3. Bipolar Disorder. *National Institute of Mental Health (NIMH).* https://www.nimh.nih.gov/health/topics/bipolar-disorder/index.shtml. Accessed April 2, 2019.

4. Mark Zuckerberg. *Forbes Media, LLC.* https://www.forbes.com/profile/mark-zuckerberg/#79ce28de3e06. Accessed April 3, 2019.

5. Elon Musk. *Forbes Media, LLC.* https://www.forbes.com/profile/elon-musk/#4c0b1d637999. Accessed April 3, 2019.

6. In: Halter JB, Ouslander JG, Studenski S, High KP, Asthana S, Supiano MA, Ritchie C. eds. Hazzard's Geriatric Medicine and Gerontology, 7e New York, NY: McGraw-Hill; . http://accessmedicine.mhmedical.com/content.aspx?bookid=1923&sectionid=143987225. Accessed February 25, 2019.

7. Balanced – Mood Disorder Support. *Meetup.* https://www.meetup.com/balanced/. Accessed April 3, 2019.

8. Valproic Acid (Oral Route). *Mayo Foundation for Medical Education and Research.* https://www.mayoclinic.org/drugs-supplements/valproic-acid-oral-route/description/drg-20072931. Accessed April 3, 2019.

9. Sandy Hook Elementary School shooting. *Encyclopedia Britannica, Inc.* https://www.britannica.com/event/newtown-shootings-of-2012. Accessed April 3, 2019. About Mental Health America.

10. *Mental Health America.* http://www.mentalhealthamerica.net/about-us. Accessed April 3, 2019. Miller, Michael Craig.

11. ASK THE DOCTOR: WHAT IS HYPOMANIA. *HARVARD MENTAL HEALTH LETTER.* DECEMBER, 2010. HTTPS://WWW.HEALTH.HARVARD.EDU/NEWSLETTER_ARTICLE/WHAT-IS-HYPOMANIA. ACCESSED APRIL 3, 2019.

12. GRUSH, LOREN. NO LONGER SILENT: MAN WITH BIPOLAR DISORDER SPEAKS UP ABOUT HIS ILLNESS, INSPIRING OTHERS. *FOX NEWS NETWORK, LLC.* HTTPS://WWW.FOXNEWS.COM/HEALTH/NO-LONGER-SILENT-MAN-WITH-BIPOLAR-DISORDER-SPEAKS-UP-ABOUT-HIS-ILLNESS-INSPIRING-OTHERS. ACCESSED APRIL 3, 2019.

13. ABOUT NAMI. *NAMI.* HTTPS://WWW.NAMI.ORG/ABOUT-NAMI. ACCESSED APRIL 3, 2019.

14. MENTAL HEALTH MATTERS DAY. *MENTAL HEALTH AMERICA OF CALIFORNIA.* HTTP://WWW.MENTALHEALTHMATTERSDAY.ORG/. ACCESSED APRIL 3, 2019.

15. SUICIDE FACTS. *SAVE.* HTTPS://SAVE.ORG/ABOUT-SUICIDE/SUICIDE-FACTS/. ACCESSED APRIL 3, 2019.

16. TAKING THE MCAT EXAM. *AAMC.* HTTPS://STUDENTS-RESIDENTS.AAMC.ORG/APPLYING-MEDICAL-SCHOOL/TAKING-MCAT-EXAM/. ACCESSED MARCH 15, 2019.

17. OBSESSIVE-COMPULSIVE DISORDER (OCD) & RELATED DISORDERS. IN: PAPADAKIS MA, MCPHEE SJ, BERNSTEIN J. EDS. *QUICK MEDICAL DIAGNOSIS & TREATMENT 2019* NEW YORK, NY: MCGRAW-HILL; . HTTP://ACCESSMEDICINE.MHMEDICAL.COM/CONTENT.ASPX?BOOKID=2566&SECTIONID=206890671. ACCESSED MARCH 01, 2019.

18. PEDIATRIC AUTOIMMUNE NEUROPSYCHIATRIC DISORDERS ASSOCIATED WITH STREPTOCOCCUS INFECTIONS. GENETIC AND RARE DISEASE INFORMATION CENTER (GARD). HTTPS://RAREDISEASES.INFO.NIH.GOV/DISEASES/7312/PEDIATRIC-AUTOIMMUNE-NEUROPSYCHIATRIC-DISORDERS-ASSOCIATED-WITH-STREPTOCOCCUS-INFECTIONS. ACCESSED MARCH 01, 2019.

19. SULFA ALLERGIES: WHAT YOU NEED TO KNOW. WEBMD LLC. HTTPS://WWW.WEBMD.COM/ALLERGIES/SULFA-ALLERGIES#1. ACCESSED MARCH 01, 2019.

20. Minniti N, Tawadrous N. Psychological Evaluation & Intervention in Acute Rehabilitation. In: Maitin IB, Cruz E. eds. CURRENT Diagnosis & Treatment: Physical Medicine & Rehabilitation New York, NY: McGraw-Hill; 2014. http://accessmedicine.mhmedical.com/content.aspx?bookid=1180&sectionid=70382832. Accessed February 25, 2019.

21. Reus VI. Psychiatric Disorders. In: Jameson J, Fauci AS, Kasper DL, Hauser SL, Longo DL, Loscalzo J. eds. Harrison's Principles of Internal Medicine, 20e New York, NY: McGraw-Hill; . http://accessmedicine.mhmedical.com/content.aspx?bookid=2129&sectionid=192533879. Accessed February 25, 2019.

22. Pollock BG, Gerretsen P, Balakumar T, Semla TP. Psychoactive Drug Therapy. In: Halter JB, Ouslander JG, Studenski S, High KP, Asthana S, Supiano MA, Ritchie C. eds. Hazzard's Geriatric Medicine and Gerontology, 7e New York, NY: McGraw-Hill; . http://accessmedicine.mhmedical.com/content.aspx?bookid=1923&sectionid=144523476. Accessed February 25, 2019.

23. Antidepressants. In: Trevor AJ, Katzung BG, Kruidering-Hall M. eds. Katzung & Trevor's Pharmacology: Examination & Board Review, 11e New York, NY: McGraw-Hill; 2015. http://accessmedicine.mhmedical.com/content.aspx?bookid=1568&sectionid=95702844. Accessed February 25, 2019. Chapter 188.

24. Traction Alopecia and Trichotillomania. In: Usatine RP, Smith MA, Chumley HS, Mayeaux EJ, Jr.. eds. *The Color Atlas of Family Medicine, 2e* New York, NY: McGraw-Hill; 2013. http://accessmedicine.mhmedical.com/content.aspx?bookid=685&sectionid=45361259. Accessed March 01, 2019.

25. Hewlett WA. Obsessive–Compulsive Disorder. In: Ebert MH, Leckman JF, Petrakis IL. eds. *Current Diagnosis & Treatment: Psychiatry, 3e* New York, NY: McGraw-Hill; . http://accessmedicine.mhmedical.com/content.aspx?bookid=2509&sectionid=200980533. Accessed March 01, 2019.

26. Attention-Deficit/Hyperactivity Disorder. *National Institute of Mental Health*, U.S. Department of Health and Human Services, www.nimh.nih.gov/health/topics/attention-deficit-hyperactivity-disorder-adhd/index.shtml. Accessed February 25, 2019.

27. L. D, B. E, E. R, Hendin H, P. C, Romer D, E.P. M, Timothy B. *Treating and Preventing Adolescent Mental Health Disorders.*; 2017.

28. Kant J, Franklin M, Andrews LW. *The Thought That Counts: A Firsthand Account of One Teenager's Experience With Obsessive-Compulsive Disorder (Adolescent Mental Health Initiative)*. Oxford University Press; 2008.

29. Burstein A, Kelsay K, Talmi A. Child & Adolescent Psychiatric Disorders & Psychosocial Aspects of Pediatrics. In: Hay, Jr. WW, Levin MJ, Deterding RR, Abzug MJ. eds. Current Diagnosis & Treatment: Pediatrics, 24e New York, NY: McGraw-Hill; . http://accessmedicine.mhmedical.com/content.aspx?bookid=2390&sectionid=189073651. Accessed February 25, 2019.

30. Burstein A, Kelsay K, Talmi A. Child & Adolescent Psychiatric Disorders & Psychosocial Aspects of Pediatrics. In: Hay, Jr. WW, Levin MJ, Deterding RR, Abzug MJ. eds. Current Diagnosis & Treatment: Pediatrics, 24e New York, NY: McGraw-Hill; . http://accessmedicine.mhmedical.com/content.aspx?bookid=2390&sectionid=189073651. Accessed February 25, 2019.

31. "Exposure and Response Prevention (ERP)." *International OCD Foundation*, iocdf.org/about-ocd/treatment/erp/. Accessed February 25, 2019.

32. Logan Noone, shooting from the hip.

33. Esfandiari NH, McPhee SJ. Thyroid Disease. In: Hammer GD, McPhee SJ. eds. Pathophysiology of Disease: An Introduction to Clinical Medicine, 8e New York, NY: McGraw-Hill; http://accessmedicine.mhmedical.com/content.aspx?bookid=2468&sectionid=198224090. Accessed February 25, 2019.

34. Betts, Jennifer. Emo Kid Style and Beliefs. LoveToKnow, Corp. https://kids.lovetoknow.com/wiki/Emo_Kid. Accessed February 28, 2019.

35. McLeod, Saul. Type A and B Personality. (2017). SimplyPsychology. https://www.simplypsychology.org/personality-a.html. Accessed February 28, 2019.

36. About Cardiac Arrest. American Heart Association, Inc. (Mar 31, 2017). https://www.heart.org/en/health-topics/cardiac-arrest/about-cardiac-arrest. Accessed February 28, 2019.

37. Raj KS, Williams N, DeBattista C. Psychiatric Disorders. In: Papadakis MA, McPhee SJ, Rabow MW. eds. Current Medical Diagnosis & Treatment 2019 New York, NY: McGraw-Hill; . http://accessmedicine.mhmedical.com/content.aspx?bookid=2449&sectionid=194576991. Accessed February 25, 2019.

38. ADD VS ADHD. *WebMD LLC*. HTTPS://WWW.WEBMD.COM/ADD-ADHD/CHILDHOOD-ADHD/ADD-VS-ADHD#1. ACCESSED MARCH 15, 2019.

39. PHILLIPS KA, BONCI A. COCAINE AND OTHER COMMONLY USED DRUGS. IN: JAMESON J, FAUCI AS, KASPER DL, HAUSER SL, LONGO DL, LOSCALZO J. EDS. HARRISON'S PRINCIPLES OF INTERNAL MEDICINE, 20E NEW YORK, NY: MCGRAW-HILL; . HTTP://ACCESSMEDICINE.MHMEDICAL.COM/CONTENT.ASPX?BOOKID=2129&SECTIONID=192534128. ACCESSED FEBRUARY 25, 2019.

40. BURSTEIN A, KELSAY K, TALMI A. CHILD & ADOLESCENT PSYCHIATRIC DISORDERS & PSYCHOSOCIAL ASPECTS OF PEDIATRICS. IN: HAY, JR. WW, LEVIN MJ, DETERDING RR, ABZUG MJ. EDS. CURRENT DIAGNOSIS & TREATMENT: PEDIATRICS, 24E NEW YORK, NY: MCGRAW-HILL; . HTTP://ACCESSMEDICINE.MHMEDICAL.COM/CONTENT.ASPX?BOOKID=2390&SECTIONID=189073651. ACCESSED FEBRUARY 25, 2019.

41. WHAT IS COGNITIVE BEHAVIORAL THERAPY? *AMERICAN PSYCHOLOGICAL ASSOCIATION*. HTTPS://WWW.APA.ORG/PTSD-GUIDELINE/PATIENTS-AND-FAMILIES/COGNITIVE-BEHAVIORAL. ACCESSED MARCH 15, 2019.

42. BURSTEIN A, KELSAY K, TALMI A. CHILD & ADOLESCENT PSYCHIATRIC DISORDERS & PSYCHOSOCIAL ASPECTS OF PEDIATRICS. IN: HAY, JR. WW, LEVIN MJ, DETERDING RR, ABZUG MJ. EDS. CURRENT DIAGNOSIS & TREATMENT: PEDIATRICS, 24E NEW YORK, NY: MCGRAW-HILL; . HTTP://ACCESSMEDICINE.MHMEDICAL.COM/CONTENT.ASPX?BOOKID=2390&SECTIONID=189073651. ACCESSED FEBRUARY 25, 2019.

43. "JETBLUE AIRWAYS CORPORATION - COMPANY PROFILE, INFORMATION, BUSINESS DESCRIPTION, HISTORY, BACKGROUND INFORMATION ON JETBLUE AIRWAYS CORPORATION." *REFERENCE FOR BUSINESS*, WWW.REFERENCEFORBUSINESS.COM/HISTORY2/38/JETBLUE-AIRWAYS-CORPORATION.HTML#IXZZ5XTOTZSZT. ACCESSED FEBRUARY 25, 2019.

44. TEAM, UNDERSTOOD. "CELEBRITY SPOTLIGHT: HOW MICHAEL PHELPS' ADHD HELPED HIM MAKE OLYMPIC HISTORY." *UNDERSTOOD.ORG*, WWW.UNDERSTOOD.ORG/EN/LEARNING-ATTENTION-ISSUES/PERSONAL-STORIES/FAMOUS-PEOPLE/CELEBRITY-SPOTLIGHT-HOW-MICHAEL-PHELPS-ADHD-HELPED-HIM-MAKE-OLYMPIC-HISTORY. ACCESSED 25 FEBRUARY 2019.

45. Pollock BG, Gerretsen P, Balakumar T, Semla TP. Psychoactive Drug Therapy. In: Halter JB, Ouslander JG, Studenski S, High KP, Asthana S, Supiano MA, Ritchie C. eds. Hazzard's Geriatric Medicine and Gerontology, 7e New York, NY: McGraw-Hill; . http://accessmedicine.mhmedical.com/content.aspx?bookid=1923&sectionid=144523476. Accessed February 25, 2019.

46. Sudafed: What you Need to Know. *Healthline Media*. https://www.healthline.com/health/allergies/sudafed#side-effects. Accessed March 20, 2019.

47. Key Findings – A closer Look at the Link Between Specific SSRIs and Birth Defects. *Centers for Disease Control and Prevention*. https://www.cdc.gov/pregnancy/meds/treatingfortwo/features/ssrisandbirthdefects.html.. Accessed March 20, 2019.

48. Alien (1979). *IMDB.com, Inc*. https://www.imdb.com/title/tt0078748/. Accessed March 20, 2019.

49. The Incredible Shrinking Brains of New Mothers. *Healthline Media*. https://www.healthline.com/health-news/pregnancy-effects-on-brain#8. Accessed March 20, 2019.

50. Meconium Aspiration Syndrome. *U.S. National Library of Medicine*. https://medlineplus.gov/ency/article/001596.htm. Accessed March 20, 2019.

51. Apgar Score. *U.S. National Library of Medicine*. https://medlineplus.gov/ency/article/003402.htm. Accessed March 20, 2019.

52. Postpartum Depression. *Mayo Foundation for Medical Education and Research*. https://www.mayoclinic.org/diseases-conditions/postpartum-depression/symptoms-causes/syc-20376617. Accessed March 20, 2019.

53. Editors of Encyclopedia Britannica. Fox Broadcasting Company. (Feb 12, 2019) https://www.britannica.com/topic/Fox-Broadcasting-Company. Accessed February 28, 2019.

54. The Wonder Years. IMDB.com, Inc. https://www.imdb.com/title/tt0094582/. Accessed February 28, 2019.

55. Thomas, Laura. Gaslight and Gaslighting. *Lancet Psychiatry, The.* Volume 5, Issue 2. Pg 117-118. Elsevier Ltd. https://www.clinicalkey.com/#!/content/journal/1-s2.0-S2215036618300245. Accessed February 25, 2019.

56. Chapter 227. Graves' Disease and Goiter. In: Usatine RP, Smith MA, Chumley HS, Mayeaux EJ, Jr.. eds. The Color Atlas of Family Medicine, 2e New York, NY: McGraw-Hill; 2013. http://accessmedicine.mhmedical.com/content.aspx?bookid=685&sectionid=45361304. Accessed February 25, 2019.

57. Jameson J, Mandel SJ, Weetman AP. Thyroid Nodular Disease and Thyroid Cancer. In: Jameson J, Fauci AS, Kasper DL, Hauser SL, Longo DL, Loscalzo J. eds. Harrison's Principles of Internal Medicine, 20e New York, NY: McGraw-Hill; . http://accessmedicine.mhmedical.com/content.aspx?bookid=2129&sectionid=188731530. Accessed February 25, 2019.

58. Beta Blockers. *Mayo Clinic*, Mayo Foundation for Medical Education and Research, 6 Apr. 2018, www.mayoclinic.org/diseases-conditions/high-blood-pressure/in-depth/beta-blockers/art-20044522. Accessed February 25, 2019.

59. Paroxetine Oral : Uses, Side Effects, Interactions, Pictures, Warnings & Dosing. *WebMD*, WebMD, www.webmd.com/drugs/2/drug-6969-9095/paroxetine-oral/paroxetine-oral/details. Accessed February 25, 2019.

60. Ativan Oral : Uses, Side Effects, Interactions, Pictures, Warnings & Dosing. *WebMD*, WebMD, www.webmd.com/drugs/2/drug-6685/ativan-oral/details. Accessed February 25, 2019.

61. Major Depressive Disorder Diagnostic Criteria - SIGE CAPS. *Family Medicine Reference*, 2 Dec. 2011, www.fammedref.org/mnemonic/major-depressive-disorder-diagnostic-criteria-sigme-caps. Accessed February 25, 2019.

62. Citalopram Oral : Uses, Side Effects, Interactions, Pictures, Warnings & Dosing. *WebMD*, WebMD, www.webmd.com/drugs/2/drug-1701/citalopram-oral/details. Accessed February 25, 2019.

63. The Reality of Imposter Syndrome. Psychology Today. Sussex Publishers, LLC. September 03, 2018. https://www.psychologytoday.com/us/blog/real-women/201809/the-reality-imposter-syndrome. Accessed March 01, 2019.

64. Laura, in a moment of reflective appreciation for her hubby.

65. Levothyroxine Oral : Uses, Side Effects, Interactions, Pictures, Warnings & Dosing. *WebMD*, WebMD, www.webmd.com/drugs/2/drug-1433/levothyroxine-oral/details. Accessed February 25, 2019.

66. Lisinopril. WebMD, LLC. https://www.webmd.com/drugs/2/drug-6873-9371/lisinopril-oral/lisinopril-oral/details. Accessed March 01, 2019.

67. Adderall Oral : Uses, Side Effects, Interactions, Pictures, Warnings & Dosing. *WebMD*, WebMD, www.webmd.com/drugs/2/drug-63163/adderall-oral/details. Accessed February 25, 2019.

68. "David Strayer - Driver Distraction." *The Effect of Context on Memory | GoCognitive*, http://gocognitive.net/interviews/david-strayer-driver-distraction. Accessed February 25, 2019.

69. EEG (Electroencephalogram). Mayo Foundation for Medical Education and Research. https://www.mayoclinic.org/tests-procedures/eeg/about/pac-20393875. Accessed March 3, 2019.

70. Williams. Florence. (2016). This is Your Brain on Nature. *National Geographic, [online] pp.49-67.* www.nationalgeographic.com/magazine/2016/01/call-to-wild/ Accessed 25 Feb 2019.

71. Strayed, Cheryl. Wild: From Lost to Found on the Pacific Crest Trail. Knopf; 2012.

72. Bupropion HCl Oral : Uses, Side Effects, Interactions, Pictures, Warnings & Dosing. *WebMD*, WebMD, www.webmd.com/drugs/2/drug-13507-155/bupropion-hcl-oral/bupropion-oral/details. Accessed February 25, 2019.

73. Psychiatric Disorders. In: Kasper DL, Fauci AS, Hauser SL, Longo DL, Jameson J, Loscalzo J. eds. *Harrison's Manual of Medicine, 19e* New York, NY: McGraw-Hill; . http://accessmedicine.mhmedical.com/content.aspx?bookid=1820&sectionid=127560439. Accessed March 01, 2019.

74. About Pave. PAVE. https://www.shatteringthesilence.org/about-us/about-pave/. Accessed March 01, 2019.

257

75. ATTENTION-DEFICIT/HYPERACTIVITY DISORDER. *NATIONAL INSTITUTE OF MENTAL HEALTH*, U.S. DEPARTMENT OF HEALTH AND HUMAN SERVICES, WWW.NIMH.NIH.GOV/HEALTH/TOPICS/ATTENTION-DEFICIT-HYPERACTIVITY-DISORDER-ADHD/INDEX.SHTML. ACCESSED FEBRUARY 25, 2019.

76. ANTIDEPRESSANTS. IN: TREVOR AJ, KATZUNG BG, KRUIDERING-HALL M. EDS. KATZUNG & TREVOR'S PHARMACOLOGY: EXAMINATION & BOARD REVIEW, 11E NEW YORK, NY: MCGRAW-HILL; 2015. HTTP://ACCESSMEDICINE.MHMEDICAL.COM/CONTENT.ASPX?BOOKID=15 68&SECTIONID=95702844. ACCESSED MARCH 26, 2019.

77. AMBIEN ORAL : USES, SIDE EFFECTS, INTERACTIONS, PICTURES, WARNINGS & DOSING. *WEBMD*, WEBMD, WWW.WEBMD.COM/DRUGS/2/DRUG-9690/AMBIEN-ORAL/DETAILS. ACCESSED FEBRUARY 25, 2019.

78. JUSTIN, ADORINGLY TO HIS WIFE.

79. IMPACT OF DSM-IV TO DSM-5 CHANGES ON NATIONAL HEALTH SURVEY ON DRUG USE AND HEALTH. *SUBSTANCE ABUSE AND MENTAL HEALTH SERVICES ADMINISTRATION*. 2016 JUNE. TABLE 3.22, DSM-IV TO DSM-5 SCHIZOPHRENIA COMPARISON. HTTPS://WWW.NCBI.NLM.NIH.GOV/BOOKS/NBK519704/TABLE/CH3.T2 2/ ACCESSED. MARCH 25, 2019.

80. THE NEW DSM-5: SCHIZOPHRENIA SPECTRUM AND OTHER PSYCHOTIC DISORDERS. C. E. ZUPANICK. *MENTALHELP.NET*. HTTPS://WWW.MENTALHELP.NET/ARTICLES/THE-NEW-DSM-5-SCHIZOPHRENIA-SPECTRUM-AND-OTHER-PSYCHOTIC-DISORDERS/. ACCESSED MARCH 25, 2019.

81. RESACA. *MERRIAM-WEBSTER, INC.* HTTPS://WWW.MERRIAM-WEBSTER.COM/DICTIONARY/RESACA. ACCESSED MARCH 15, 2019.

82. PARANOIA AND DELUSIONAL DISORDERS. *MENTAL HEALTH AMERICA.* HTTP://WWW.MENTALHEALTHAMERICA.NET/CONDITIONS/PARANOIA-AND-DELUSIONAL-DISORDERS. ACCESSED MARCH 15, 2019.

83. SCHIZOPHRENIA. *NATIONAL INSTITUTE OF MENTAL HEALTH.* HTTPS://WWW.NIMH.NIH.GOV/HEALTH/TOPICS/SCHIZOPHRENIA/INDE X.SHTML. ACCESSED MARCH 15, 2019.

84. PARANOID PERSONALITY DISORDER. *MEDLINEPLUS.* HTTPS://MEDLINEPLUS.GOV/ENCY/ARTICLE/000938.HTM. ACCESSED MARCH 25, 2019.

85. MACHISMO. *MERRIAM-WEBSTER, INC.* HTTPS://WWW.MERRIAM-WEBSTER.COM/DICTIONARY/MACHISMO. ACCESSED MARCH 15, 2019.

86. CATARACTS. *MAYO FOUNDATION FOR MEDICAL EDUCATION AND RESEARCH*. HTTPS://WWW.MAYOCLINIC.ORG/DISEASES-CONDITIONS/CATARACTS/SYMPTOMS-CAUSES/SYC-20353790. ACCESSED MARCH 15, 2019.

87. DIABETES. *MEDLINEPLUS*. U.S. NATIONAL LIBRARY OF MEDICINE. HTTPS://MEDLINEPLUS.GOV/DIABETES.HTML. ACCESSED MARCH 15, 2019.

88. EXERCISE AND DEPRESSION. *WEBMD LLC*. HTTPS://WWW.WEBMD.COM/DEPRESSION/GUIDE/EXERCISE-DEPRESSION#1. ACCESSED MARCH 15, 2019.

89. TAKING THE MCAT EXAM. *AAMC*. HTTPS://STUDENTS-RESIDENTS.AAMC.ORG/APPLYING-MEDICAL-SCHOOL/TAKING-MCAT-EXAM/. ACCESSED MARCH 15, 2019.

I'm a medical student who lives with bipolar disorder. The mission of my podcast is to help listeners feel more comfortable discussing mental health. I share my own experiences and thoughts, and I interview mental health advocates who have influenced me. My life is easier living openly about my mental health, and I want to convince you to live the same way.

**TALK MENTAL HEALTH WITH LOGAN NOONE**

*Available on iTunes; Spotify; iHeartRadio; Stitcher; or wherever you listen to podcasts.*

Made in the USA
San Bernardino, CA
12 May 2019